A George Orwell Chronology

Author Chronologies

General Editor: **Norman Page**, Emeritus Professor of Modern English Literature, University of Nottingham

Published titles include:

J. L. Bradley
A RUSKIN CHRONOLOGY

Gordon Campbell
A MILTON CHRONOLOGY

Martin Garrett
A BROWNING CHRONOLOGY:
ELIZABETH BARRETT BROWNING AND ROBERT BROWNING

A. M. Gibbs
A BERNARD SHAW CHRONOLOGY

J. R. Hammond
A ROBERT LOUIS STEVENSON CHRONOLOGY
AN EDGAR ALLAN POE CHRONOLOGY
AN H. G. WELLS CHRONOLOGY
A GEORGE ORWELL CHRONOLOGY

John McDermott
A HOPKINS CHRONOLOGY

Norman Page
AN EVELYN WAUGH CHRONOLOGY

Peter Preston
A D. H. LAWRENCE CHRONOLOGY

Author Chronologies Series
Series Standing Order ISBN 0-333-71484-9
(*outside North America only*)

You can receive future titles in this series as they are published by placing a standing order. Please contact your bookseller or, in case of difficulty, write to us at the address below with your name and address, the title of the series and the ISBN quoted above.

Customer Services Department, Macmillan Distribution Ltd, Houndmills, Basingstoke, Hampshire RG21 6XS, England

A George Orwell Chronology

J. R. Hammond
Research Fellow
Nottingham Trent University

palgrave

© J. R. Hammond 2000

All rights reserved. No reproduction, copy or transmission of this publication may be made without written permission.

No paragraph of this publication may be reproduced, copied or transmitted save with written permission or in accordance with the provisions of the Copyright, Designs and Patents Act 1988, or under the terms of any licence permitting limited copying issued by the Copyright Licensing Agency, 90 Tottenham Court Road, London W1P 0LP.

Any person who does any unauthorised act in relation to this publication may be liable to criminal prosecution and civil claims for damages.

The author has asserted his right to be identified as the author of this work in accordance with the Copyright, Designs and Patents Act 1988.

First published 2000 by
PALGRAVE
Houndmills, Basingstoke, Hampshire RG21 6XS and
175 Fifth Avenue, New York, N. Y. 10010
Companies and representatives throughout the world

PALGRAVE is the new global academic imprint of
St. Martin's Press LLC Scholarly and Reference Division and
Palgrave Publishers Ltd (formerly Macmillan Press Ltd).

ISBN 0-333-76033-6

This book is printed on paper suitable for recycling and made from fully managed and sustained forest sources.

A catalogue record for this book is available from the British Library.

Library of Congress Cataloging-in-Publication Data
Hammond, J. R. (John R.), 1933–
  A George Orwell chronology / J.R. Hammond.
    p. cm. — (Author chronologies)
  Includes bibliographical references and index.
  ISBN 0-333-76033-6
  1. Orwell, George, 1903-1950—Chronology. 2. Authors, English—20th century—Chronology. I. Title. II. Series.
PR6029.R8 Z677 2000
828'.91209—dc21
[B]
                                                              00-059124

10 9 8 7 6 5 4 3 2 1
09 08 07 06 05 04 03 02 01 00

Printed and bound in Great Britain by
Antony Rowe Ltd, Chippenham, Wiltshire

'He had the gift, he had the courage, he had the persistence to go on in spite of failure, sickness, poverty, and opposition, until he became an acknowledged master of English prose.'
Ruth Pitter

'I was a stage rebel, Orwell a true one.'
Cyril Connolly

'If you want to understand Orwell, you have to understand Blair.'
Richard Rees

Contents

General Editor's Preface	ix
Introduction	xi
Acknowledgements	xix
The Blair Family	xx
A GEORGE ORWELL CHRONOLOGY	1
The Orwell Circle	95
Chronology of Orwell's Works	109
Orwell's London: A Chronology	111
Nineteen Eighty-Four: A Chronology	113
Sources	115
Index	117

General Editor's Preface

Most biographies are ill adapted to serve as works of reference – not surprisingly so, since the biographer is likely to regard his function as the devising of a continuous and readable narrative, with excursions into interpretation and speculation, rather than a bald recital of facts. There are times, however, when anyone reading for business or pleasure needs to check a point quickly or to obtain a rapid overview of part of an author's life or career; and at such moments turning over the pages of a biography can be a time-consuming and frustrating occupation. The present series of volumes aims at providing a means whereby the chronological facts of an author's life and career, rather than needing to be prised out of the narrative in which they are (if they appear at all) securely embedded, can be seen at a glance. Moreover, whereas biographies are often, and quite understandably, vague over matters of fact (since it makes for tediousness to be forever enumerating details of dates and places), a chronology can be precise whenever it is possible to be precise.

Thanks to the survival, sometimes in very large quantities, of letters, diaries, notebooks and other documents, as well as to thoroughly researched biographies and bibliographies, this material now exists in abundance for many major authors. In the case of, for example, Dickens, we can often ascertain what he was doing in each month and week, and almost on each day, of his prodigiously active working life; and the student of, say, *David Copperfield* is likely to find it fascinating as well as useful to know just when Dickens was at work on each part of that novel, what other literary enterprises he was engaged in at the same time, whom he was meeting, what places he was visiting, and what were the relevant circumstances of his personal and professional life. Such a chronology is not, of course, a substitute for a biography; but its arrangement, in combination with its index, makes it a much more convenient tool for this kind of purpose; and it may be acceptable as a form of 'alternative' biography, with its own distinctive advantages as well as its obvious limitations. Since information relating to an author's early years is usually scanty and chronologically imprecise, the opening section of some volumes in this series groups together the years of childhood and adolescence. Thereafter each year, and usually each month, is dealt with separately. Information not readily assignable to a specific month or day is given as a general note under the relevant year or month. The first entry for each month carries an indication of the day of the week, so that when necessary this can be readily calculated for other dates. Each volume also contains a bibliography of the principal sources of information. In the chronology itself, the sources of many of the more specific items, including quotations, are identified, in order that the reader who wishes to do so may consult the original contexts.

NORMAN PAGE

Introduction

George Orwell is now acknowledged as one of the most significant prose writers of the twentieth century. As novelist, essayist, and author of a number of outstanding works of reportage, he has exercised an influence on modern thought which is increasingly being recognised. Though he died at the age of 46 he achieved world-wide fame during his lifetime and since his death his stature has grown immeasurably. Today he belongs to that select company of writers – including Lawrence, Joyce and Kafka – who have made a permanent contribution to modern literature.

An essentially private man – he could be aloof and taciturn in certain moods and had few really close friendships – he requested in his will that no biography of him should be written. This request may have been prompted by a natural reticence, or possibly by a feeling that he had himself told all that was necessary of his life story in the autobiographical section of *The Road to Wigan Pier*. But such an odd request is entirely in keeping with his quixotic temperament. He was a man who 'kept himself to himself', who attached little importance to material possessions and felt that his life was of value only in the sense that he was a writer. To him his literary work came before all else: before personal friendships, before his marriage, before his own health and happiness. 'Writing a book', he observed, 'is a horrible, exhausting struggle, like a long bout of some painful illness. One would never undertake such a thing if one were not driven on by some demon whom one can neither resist nor understand.' He was indeed driven by a demon: a consuming passion to write which indirectly contributed to his death but which has earned for him a place alongside the great radical writers of the past.

Commenting apropos Edgar Allan Poe – another writer who died at an early age and whose life was dominated by ill health – Philip Van Doren Stern observed: 'He paid dearly for immortality, gave his whole life to attain it. But in his terms it was probably worth the cost.' Much the same might be said of Orwell. One thinks of him struggling valiantly to finish *Nineteen Eighty-Four* while dying of tuberculosis, refusing to concede defeat. In common with Poe he was often miserably paid for his work yet today, ironically, his name is known and respected throughout the literary world and his books command a readership of millions.

His life was a mass of contradictions. He was successively a tramp, a schoolmaster, a village-shopkeeper, a soldier, a radio producer and a sergeant in the Home Guard. He became a political writer of uncommon ability, an essayist in the tradition of Cobbett and Defoe and an outspoken commentator on the social and political issues of his time. He was also a man who was essentially English, a man who disliked twentieth-century technology and wrote with simple feeling on gardening, wildlife and the passing of the seasons. A radical Socialist, he loved the quirkiness of such institutions as the Church of England and the monarchy. He was an old Etonian, yet wished to be accepted on equal terms by down-and-outs and the miners of Wigan.

What is the significance of Blair's assumption of a *nom de plume*? It is important because the name itself and his adoption of it have been the subject of much critical speculation. The pseudonym was chosen with surprising casualness. In November 1932, when his first book *Down and Out in Paris and London* was already in proof, the name had still not been chosen. He wrote diffidently to his agent suggesting that the book should be published pseudonymously. Too much should not be read into the choice of the name itself. It is true that 'George' has an Englishness about it, suggesting plain speaking and common sense, and that 'Orwell' was the name of a river he was fond of, but it has to be remembered that the name was selected by Gollancz from a short list submitted by Blair; the publisher might equally well have chosen 'Kenneth Miles' or 'H. Lewis Allways'. What mattered to Blair was not the name as such but the second self that the name suggested and made possible; by adopting a pseudonym he symbolically turned his back on his previous existence and assumed a new persona.

It is clear that he disliked his own name 'Eric'. He disliked the name not only because he assumed it was Scottish in origin and he had a lifelong antipathy to Scottish names and authors, but also because it reminded him of the hero of *Eric, or Little by Little* by Frederic W. Farrar, a sentimental novel which he loathed.

The adoption of a *nom de plume* enabled him to sever himself from these associations and to assume a completely different identity, that of a writer. It also enabled him to maintain a distinction between his private and his literary life. In private he was still Eric Blair; in public he was the author George Orwell. When, towards the end of his life, Anthony Powell asked him if he had ever considered legally adopting his pen-name, he replied: 'Well, I have, but then, of course, I'd have to *write* under another name if I did.'

The distinction between the two aspects of his life was important to him. (In practice it was not always possible to maintain a neat separation between the two. Friends who had known him prior to 1933 continued to call him 'Eric'; many who knew him only after his fame called him 'George'.) The point of real importance to any understanding of Orwell as a man and as a writer is this: that which had been adopted at first simply as a pen-name and with no deeper significance gradually became an actual second identity, a name synonymous with honesty, forthrightness and a militant radical attitude. The change did not happen quickly; for two or three years Blair eased himself into his new identity, writing, talking, and even dressing to conform to his new image. By 1936 the transformation was complete.

The assumption of the name George Orwell meant that he could, symbolically and actually, sever himself from his past. St Cyprian's, Eton and Burma now belonged to a phase of his life he regarded as alien. He rejected that way of life and all that it represented. He wanted passionately to opt out of the life of a gentleman and assume instead the mantle of a writer.

Despite his wish that no biography of him should be written, several full-length studies have been attempted, most notably those by Bernard Crick and Michael Shelden. Comprehensive though these are, it is arguable that no fully satisfactory biography of Orwell has yet appeared, simply because he was such a complex figure who never wholly resolved the competing tensions in his psychology. Embedded deep within his make-up was a profound pessimism which inhibited him from close friendships and darkened the closing years of his life. The only individual who succeeded in breaking through this defensive crust was his first wife, Eileen, who understood him fully and appreciated the complex forces which had made him what he was. She and she alone had the ability to see through his moods and penetrate to the 'crystal spirit' which lay beneath.

His life is reasonably well documented, partly because he was such a prolific correspondent, but inevitably the record is much fuller once he became established as a professional writer. One would like to know much more about his early life, especially his schooling at St Cyprian's. What was the truth about this? If his own testimony is to be believed (in 'Such, Such were the Joys'), it was a dreadful establishment, only a little removed from Dotheboys Hall in Dickens's *Nicholas Nickleby*. Michael Shelden, on the other hand, has unearthed evidence suggesting that this picture may be distorted and that the school was not nearly so bad as Orwell leads us to believe. The point is of some significance as a body of criticism has arisen implying that the torture and cruelty of *Nineteen Eighty-Four* had its roots at St Cyprian's. Again, what impact did the years at Eton have upon him? And how influential was the Eton experience in determining his attitude to manual workers?

One would also like to know much more about his thoughts and actions during the years 1927–32 when he was striving to embark on a literary career and writing successive versions of *Down and Out* and *Burmese Days*. And we still know tantalisingly little about his reading and writing during his years in Burma, nor why he made the crucial choice to enter the Imperial Police instead of going on to university.

The period covered by his life, 1903–50, is one of exceptional interest, in that it was both an age of fundamental social and political change and also one of violent intellectual ferment. He was born before the aeroplane, when the motor car was a rarity, television and computers were unknown and world war was almost unthinkable. The years he spent at preparatory school were lived against the background of the First World War with its terrible carnage and social upheaval. In the same month in which his first book was published, January 1933, Hitler became Chancellor of Germany.

The years in which he was finding himself as a writer, 1933–6, were years of immense social change in Britain. It was a period of mounting unemployment, widespread poverty, and rising social unrest. In the year in which *The Road to Wigan Pier* was written, 1936, unemployment in Britain rose to three million. In that same year, the Spanish Civil War erupted, polarising radical opinion in Britain and Europe into diametrically opposed camps. Simultaneously, totalitarian regimes were spreading across Europe, accompanied by violence and cruelty on an unprecedented scale, and the persecution of minorities. Three years later still came the Second World War, bringing in its train immense social and political changes and the onset of the use of nuclear weapons.

It was also an age of intense ideological ferment. It is difficult for us today – living, as we do, in an age of doubt and ambiguity – to recapture the passionate certainties of political debate in the 1930s. The decade was one of fierce argument on the pros and cons of democracy, socialism, communism, fascism, anarchism and pacifism. In such an atmosphere it was difficult if not impossible to be neutral. Whatever one's political stance, one was inevitably caught up in these ideological debates; one took sides. Orwell was no exception. The very titles of the journals to which he contributed recall the heated atmosphere of those times: *Polemic, Partisan Review, Controversy, Revolt, Left Forum*. In his famous essay 'Why I Write' he defined his literary philosophy in these terms: 'I write because there is some lie that I want to expose, some fact to which I want to draw attention, and my initial concern is to get a hearing.' He was, before all else, a *political* writer, passionately concerned about the betterment of the human condition. If today much of his writing seems fiercely partisan, this has to be balanced against his lifelong concern for the truth: in such essays as 'Politics and the English Language', 'The Prevention of Literature', and 'Propaganda and Demotic Speech', he insisted on the need for the utmost clarity of expression and for striving towards honesty in written and spoken expression.

His life is also of unusual interest in that it impinged on so many literary figures of his time: Arthur Koestler, Henry Miller, H. G. Wells, T. S. Eliot, Cyril Connolly, John Middleton Murry, Anthony Powell and Stephen Spender were all affected to greater or lesser degree by Orwell. As a novelist and journalist, Orwell encountered many of the editors, publishers and critics of his day and their names inevitably figure in any study of his times. He was so closely involved in the literary and political issues of his age that a chronology of his life is, in a sense, a survey of the history of radical thought in the first half of the twentieth century.

I hope that this *Chronology* will be found useful by those readers who wish to check a point quickly without recourse to the full-scale biographies – which in any case do not always agree with one another. With its aid, the reader will be able to find answers to such questions as: At what stage in his life did Blair adopt the pseudonym George Orwell? How much time did he actually spend in Wigan? When was *Coming up for Air* written? How long did it take him to write *Animal Farm*? When did he start writing *Nineteen Eighty-Four*? How long did he live on the island of Jura? A chronology of this kind cannot be a substitute for a detailed biographical study but it can serve a useful purpose by simply presenting facts without any attempt to interpret them or place them within a psychological framework. In seeking a closer understanding of his life, we inevitably come closer to understanding Orwell the man.

H. G. Wells once remarked 'I do not see, myself, why the particulars of an author's life need be recorded.' Surely the details of a writer's life *are* of intrinsic interest, simply because life so often illuminates art. To anyone studying Orwell, it is surely of interest and relevance to know that he served five years in the Indian Imperial Police, that he spent long periods living among down and outs, that he was once a bookshop assistant and that for a time he was a schoolmaster. Orwell seems to me a classic example of a writer whose life is inextricably interwoven with his work, and in practice it is difficult if not impossible to separate the two. His novels, essays and documentaries could not have been written without a rich diversity of experience in England, Burma, France and Spain. All his experiences contributed to the man and writer he became: the Orwell who wrote *Down and Out in Paris and London* had his roots in the Eric Blair who went to school at Eton and could see life from the point of view of both a tramp and a gentleman.

Among many unanswered questions posed by his life, the central one is perhaps the most intriguing paradox of all: which among his many selves was the *real* Orwell, the essential man? Was it the rather shy figure who loved the simple life and longed to be a village shopkeeper, pottering about his cottage and garden engaged in country pursuits? Or was it the radical writer, the iconoclast who delighted in exposing falsehoods and advocated revolutionary change in society? We will never know which of these was the true Orwell; perhaps in the end it does not matter. What *does* matter is that he left a literary inheritance which has continuing relevance for us as we enter a new millennium. His books and essays continue to speak to us.

There are many questions which scholars will continue to debate. Was he on the whole an optimistic or a pessimistic writer? Was he a genuinely radical thinker or simply anxious to conserve the best of the past? To these and other questions there can be no final answers. All that can be said with confidence is that his work belongs in one of the central traditions of English letters, and that future generations will honour him for his straightforwardness and lack of pretension in an age of cynicism.

Reflecting on his life and achievement, one cannot but regret that his life was cut short at the age of 46, when he was clearly at the height of his powers and had so much still to give. Had he lived, he would assuredly have produced more novels, essays and documentaries in that inimitable style and continued to write articles commenting trenchantly on the issues of the day. Yet despite the brevity of his writing career, the volume and diversity of his achievement is remarkable. When one reflects on the power of his writings, their incisive intelligence, their outspokenness and abundant humanity, one realises that comparisons with Swift, Defoe and Voltaire are not unjustified. He was one of the few writers of this century to awaken his readers to a sense of the beauty of language and the corrupting effects of its misuse; to create a vision of human fraternity and of the misery caused by poverty and deprivation; to insist on tolerance, justice and decency in human relationships; to warn against the increasing artificiality of urban civilisation. Above all, he presented a devastating critique of totalitarianism, warning with eloquence and anger of erosions of liberty and helping his readers to recognise tyranny in all its forms. For this, and for the shining honesty of his prose, posterity has reason to be grateful.

J. R. HAMMOND

Acknowledgements

I wish to thank the General Editor of the *Author Chronologies* series, Professor Norman Page, and Charmian Hearne of Macmillan for their encouragement and counsel. I would also like to thank the staff of the following libraries for their courtesy and assistance: University College London, George Orwell Archive; National Newspaper Library, Colindale; and Nottingham Trent University. Special thanks are due to the staff of the Orwell Archive at University College London for their courtesy and helpfulness over a long period.

My warm thanks are due to Joy Bremer for typing my manuscript with her usual care, and to my wife Jean for helping with many secretarial chores, including the arduous task of working out the days of the week.

My final acknowledgement must be to Orwell himself, for the immense pleasure his writings have given to me over many years: his life is a most inspiring example of triumph over adversity.

J. R. HAMMOND

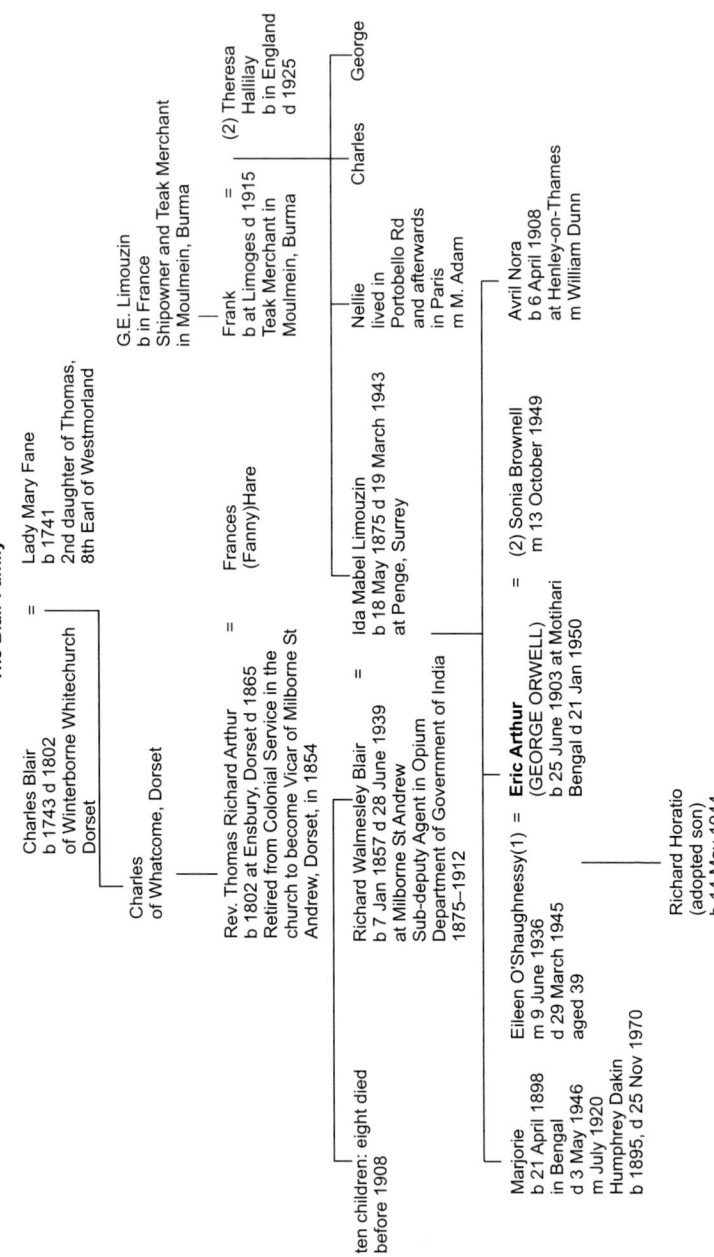

A George Orwell Chronology

[Part One: Eric Blair]

1903

June

25 (Thurs) Eric Arthur Blair is born at Motihari, Bengal, the son of Richard Walmesley Blair and Ida Mabel Blair, née Limouzin, who had married in 1896. A sister, Marjorie Frances, had been born in 1898. Richard Blair is an official in the Opium Department of the Indian Civil Service.

1904

In the summer of 1904 the Blairs come to England on leave, Richard Blair returning in the autumn to India. Ida Blair and the children settle at Henley-on-Thames, Oxfordshire.

1905

September

25 (Mon) Birth of Eileen Maud O'Shaughnessy, later to become Eric Blair's wife.

27 The Blair family move to Ermadale, Vicarage Road, Henley.

1908

April

The Blair family move to The Nutshell, Western Road, Henley.

6   (Mon) Birth of Eric Blair's sister Avril Nora.

September

Enrols as a pupil at Sunnylands, Henley, an Anglican Convent school, where Marjorie is already a pupil.

1911

May

In the spring of this year Mrs Blair enters Eric Blair as a pupil at St Cyprian's, Eastbourne, a private preparatory school (now demolished). He is to commence in September.

June

25   (Sun) Eric Blair's 8th birthday. His mother presents him with a copy of Swift's *Gulliver's Travels*.

September

Enters boarding school at St Cyprian's, Eastbourne. The head teachers are Mr and Mrs Vaughan Wilkes. Here he remains until December 1916, studying Latin, French, History, English and Arithmetic. He later records his impressions of the school in the essay 'Such, Such were the Joys'.

14 (Thurs) Writes first letter home to his mother.

October

8 (Sun) Writes to his mother, the first of many letters giving her his weekly placings in Arithmetic, Latin and History.

December

His childhood reading up to this time has included *Gulliver's Travels*, *Tom Sawyer*, *The Coral Island* and *Rebecca of Sunnybrook Farm*. He has also read Beatrix Potter's *The Tale of Pigling Bland*.

1912

January

Richard Walmesley Blair (father) retires from the Indian Civil Service and returns to England.

August

Spends summer holidays at Polperro, Cornwall.

September

At about this time the Blair family move to Roselawn, Station Road, Shiplake (a village two miles south of Henley).

Commences second year at St Cyprian's. During this year becomes a member of the Cadet Corps Band.

1913

September

Commences third year at St Cyprian's and enters the scholarship class, beginning intensive preparation for entry to a Public School.

Cyril Connolly enters St Cyprian's and meets Eric Blair; the beginning of a lifelong friendship.

1914

August

4 (Tues) Britain declares war on Germany. First World War commences.

September

Early in the month meets the Buddicom family for the first time at Thatched Cottage, Shiplake. He befriends Jacintha Buddicom, her brother Prosper and her sister Guinever. They continue to be close friends until 1922, regularly spending school holidays together. Jacintha later records her impressions of Eric Blair in her book *Eric and Us* (1974).

Commences fourth year at St Cyprian's.

October

2 (Fri) 'Awake! Young Men of England' in *Henley and South Oxfordshire Standard*.

1915

July

Praised by his tutor for 'very promising work' in the scholarship class. Awarded the school's English prize.

September

At about this time the Blair family move to 36 St Mark's Road, Henley. Eric Blair commences final year at St Cyprian's.

1916

February

Sits scholarship examination for entry to Wellington College.

June

5 (Mon) Death of Lord Kitchener. The pupils are invited to submit a poem or essay marking the event.

10 *The Times* publishes the list of examination results for entry to Eton. Eric Blair is fourteenth, not quite high enough for entry in the autumn of 1916.

July

15 (Sat) First runner-up in the Harrow History Prize (won by Cyril Connolly).

21 'Kitchener' in *Henley and South Oxfordshire Standard*.

December

Leaves St Cyprian's for the last time. At the end of his final term receives favourable reports in Greek, Latin, French and English.

His childhood reading has included the Father Brown stories of G. K. Chesterton, the detective stories of Conan Doyle and R. Austin Freeman, and the Raffles stories of E. W. Hornung. Has also read Henry James's *The Turn of the Screw*, E. F. Benson's *The Room in the Tower*, the ghost stories of M. R. James, H. G. Wells's *A Modern Utopia* and *The Country of the Blind and Other Stories*, and Compton Mackenzie's *Sinister Street*. His favourite authors are Wells, Kipling, Wodehouse, Ian Hay, Thackeray and Swift.

1917

January

Spends one term as a pupil at Wellington College, a public school near Wokingham, Berkshire, living in Blucher Dormitory.

March

Leaves Wellington College in late March.

May

Enters Eton College as a King's Scholar (until December 1921) studying Divinity, Latin, Greek, French, English, Mathematics and Science.

As a King's Scholar he is a member of 'College', consisting of 70 scholars housed in the oldest buildings at Eton, as distinct from the Oppidans, 900 boys living in various Houses in the town.

His friends at Eton include K. S. (later Sir Steven) Runciman, Denys King-Farlow and Cyril Connolly.

August

Spends summer holidays with the Buddicom children at Ticklerton Court, Church Stretton, Shropshire.

September

Richard Walmesley Blair (father) is commissioned as a second lieutenant in the Army and posted to Marseilles. Ida Blair moves to a flat at 23 Cromwell Crescent, Earls Court, and takes a clerical post at the Ministry of Pensions.

December

Spends Christmas holidays with the Buddicom family at Shiplake.

1918

January

At about this time writes a short story, 'The Vernon Murders', and a play, 'The Man and the Maid'.

June

3 (Mon) Publishes four contributions in *The Election Times*, a

handwritten student journal: 'The Wounded Cricketer', 'The Slack Bob', 'The Adventure of the Lost Meat-Card' and 'A Peep into the Future'.

September

Writes poem 'The Pagan' for Jacintha Buddicom.

Commences second year at Eton.

28   (Sat) Plays the wall game for first time.

November

Confirmed into the Church of England by Rev. Charles Gore, Bishop of Oxford.

11   (Mon) Armistice signed. End of First World War.

December

17   (Tues) To Shiplake to spend Christmas holidays with the Buddicom family.

1919

September

Commences third year at Eton.

Becomes a 'General Division specialist', concentrating on Divinity, Geography, Ancient History, French, Shakespeare and Latin.

December

Richard Walmesley Blair (father) is demobilised and returns home.

25 (Thurs) Presents Jacintha Buddicom with a copy of *Dracula*.

1920

April

1 (Thurs) 'Ode to Field Days' in *College Days*.

7–30 Spends Easter holiday with the Buddicoms at Shiplake.

June

Presents a copy of Bernard Shaw's *Misalliance* to the College Reading Room.

27 (Sun) Asks Mrs Buddicom for permission to watch Henley regatta from her punt.

30 At Henley.

July

Marjorie Blair (sister) marries Humphrey Dakin.

Eric Blair spends part of summer holiday at 5 Horseshoes, Maidensgrove (near Henley), and part at Polperro, Cornwall.

9 (Fri) 'Is There Any Truth in Spiritualism?' and 'The Millionaire's Pearl' in *College Days*.

August

9 (Mon) To Ticklerton to spend August with the Buddicoms.

September

4 (Sat) Returns to his parents in London.

17 Sees Galsworthy's *The Skin Game*.

17 Returns to Eton.

October

6 (Wed) Scores spectacular goal in wall game.

December

20 (Mon) To Natural History Museum and Olympia Fair with Prosper Buddicom.

28 Attends performance of *The Blue Lagoon* at the Prince of Wales Theatre, Coventry Street, W1.

29 Sees *The Beggars Opera* at the Lyric, Hammersmith.

30 To Walnut Tree House, Burstall, Ipswich, for the remainder of the holiday.

1921

July

27 (Wed) Elected a member of the College Debating Society.

August

Spends summer holiday at Glencroft, Rickmansworth, with his mother, Avril Blair (sister) and the Buddicoms. Presents Jacintha Buddicom with a copy of Milton's poems.

September

Commences his final term at Eton, in the Sixth Form.

October

13 (Thurs) Recites an extract from R. L. Stevenson's 'The Suicide Club' at a formal speech day.

29 Becomes member of College wall game team.

November

27 (Sun) Receives his colours for wall game.

30 Takes part in wall game, Collegers versus Oppidans.

December

Richard Walmesley Blair (father) and Ida Blair move to 40 Stradbroke Road, Southwold, Suffolk.

20 (Tues) Leaves Eton for the last time and travels to Southwold.

His reading at Eton has included Housman's *A Shropshire Lad*, Wilde's *The Picture of Dorian Gray*, Jack London's *The People of the Abyss* and *The Call of the Wild*, M. R. James's *Ghost Stories of an Antiquary*, Kipling's *Kim*, and the short stories of Edgar Allan Poe. He has also read some of D. H. Lawrence's poetry.

1922

January

Begins studying for examinations for entry to Indian Imperial Police, attending cramming classes in Southwold.

He studies English, English History, Mathematics, French, Latin, Greek and Drawing.

June

27 (Tues) Sits first of examinations at the Civil Service Commission, London, for entry to Indian Imperial Police. The examinations are held over an eight-day period.

July

4 (Tues) Sits final examination. In total he receives 8,463 out of a possible 12,400 marks.

September

Passes horse riding test.

October

27 (Fri) Sails from Birkenhead to Rangoon on the S. S. *Herefordshire* to take up appointment as Probationary Assistant Superintendent of Police.

November

26? (Sun) Arrives at Rangoon.

28 Boards mail train from Rangoon to Mandalay.

29 Arrives at Mandalay and reports to the Police Training School. Commences a nine months' course at the School, studying Law, Languages, Accounts and Police Procedure.

1924

January

25 (Fri) Final day at Mandalay Police Training School.

26 Posted to Myaungmya, a district headquarters in the Irrawaddy Delta, 80 miles west of Rangoon.

His duties include supervising stores of ammunition and equipment, training locally recruited constables, organising night patrols, overseeing local police stations, supervising the investigation of minor crimes and deputising for his superior officers in their absence.

May

31 (Sat) Posted to Twante, further east in the Delta, as Sub-Divisional Police Officer. Here he spends much of his time on tour, in charge of several police stations.

June

25 (Wed) Eric Blair's 21st birthday.

December

16 (Tues) Posted to Syriam, the headquarters of the Hanthawaddy District. His probation is now at an end:

he is appointed Assistant District Superintendent. His main responsibility is to oversee the security of the oil refinery.

1925

September

26 (Sat) Posted to Insein, 10 miles north of Rangoon, where he is in charge of District Headquarters.

1926

April

19 (Mon) Posted to Moulmein, the third largest city in Burma. Here he has nearly 300 men under his command.

December

23 (Thurs) Posted to Katha in Upper Burma, 200 miles north of Mandalay, as Headquarters Assistant.

1927

June

Applies for leave, ostensibly on medical grounds. He is granted eight months' leave, with effect from 1 July.

30 (Thurs) Final day at Katha.

July

1 (Fri) Leaves Katha by train bound for Rangoon.

14 Sails for England on the MV *Shropshire*.

His reading during the years in Burma has included Tolstoy's *War and Peace*, Samuel Butler's *Notebooks*, D. H. Lawrence's *Women in Love* and *The Prussian Officer*, and works by Poe, Mark Twain and Maugham.

August

En route for home, spends some time in Marseilles (where he witnesses a demonstration protesting against the execution of the alleged anarchists Sacco and Vanzetti), then returns to England via Paris, reaching Southwold in late August.

At about this time Eric Blair's parents move to 3 Queen Street, Southwold.

September

On holiday in Polperro with his parents and sisters. Decides to resign permanently from Indian Imperial Police.

October

Spends two weeks at Ticklerton, Shropshire, then moves to London, where he finds cheap lodgings at 22 Portobello Road, Notting Hill. Here he is a neighbour of Ruth Pitter and Kathleen O'Hara. Spends the autumn and winter writing short stories and poetry; goes on tramping expeditions in the East End of London.

November

26 (Sat) Submits formal letter of resignation from Imperial Police. At the end of the month the Home Department of the Government of India sends a telegram to the India Office: 'E. A. Blair, India Police, Burma, who joined on 27 November 1922, and is on leave in England up to 12 March 1928, has applied for permission to resign from 1st January next. Government of Burma recommends acceptance. We agree.'

December

Learns that his resignation has been accepted.

1928

January

1 (Sun) Official date of resignation from Indian Imperial Police.

April

Moves to Paris and takes up residence at 6 Rue du Pot de Fer, on the Left Bank (later described as Rue de Coq d'Or in *Down and Out in Paris and London*). Continues to work on short stories and poems. Begins early drafts of *Down and Out in Paris and London* and *Burmese Days*, the latter under the title 'The Tale of John Flory'.

October

6 (Sat) 'La Censure en Angleterre' in *Monde*, his first published article as a professional writer.

December

28 (Fri) The first of three articles on the plight of the British worker in *Progrès Civique*.

29 'A Farthing Newspaper' in *GK's Weekly*.

1929

January

4 (Fri) 'A Day in the Life of a Tramp' in *Progrès Civique*.

11 'The Beggars of London' in *Progrès Civique*.

February

19 (Tues) The literary agent L. I. Bailey (employed by the McClure Newspaper Syndicate) tells Blair he wishes to see more of his work. Blair submits some short stories, adding he has a book on 'Tramps and Beggars' in preparation.

March

7 (Thurs)–22 Admitted to the Hôpital Cochin, Paris, suffering from bronchitis. Here he remains for two weeks, an experience later described in 'How the Poor Die'.

23 'John Galsworthy' in *Monde*.

28 Bailey confirms receipt of short stories.

April

29 (Mon) Bailey rejects most of the short stories but commends 'The Man in Kid Gloves'.

May

4 (Sat) 'Comment on Exploite un Peuple' in *Progrès Civique*.

June

Bailey tells Eric Blair he has failed to place 'The Man in Kid Gloves'.

August

Submits first version of 'The Spike' to *Adelphi*.

September

22 (Sun) Asks *Adelphi* if they wish to publish 'The Spike'.

October

Employed as a *plongeur* (dishwasher) at the Hotel Lotti during October, November and early December, working 13 hours a day, later described in chapters 10–22 of *Down and Out in Paris and London*.

28 Collapse of US Stock Exchange precipitates world economic crisis.

December

12 (Thurs) Agrees to *Adelphi*'s terms for publication of 'The Spike'.

Returns to England in time for Christmas. Joins his parents at Southwold.

1930

March

Reviews Lewis Mumford's *Herman Melville* in *Adelphi*.

Stays with his sister Marjorie Blair and her husband Humphrey Dakin at Bramley, Yorkshire (until June), working on a draft of *Down and Out in Paris and London* under the title 'A Scullion's Diary'.

June

Reviews Edith Sitwell's *Alexander Pope* in *Adelphi*.

Returns to Southwold. Accepts post as tutor-companion for the three school-aged sons of Mr and Mrs C. R. Peters.

October

Reviews J. B. Priestley's *Angel Pavement* in *Adelphi*.

Finishes draft of *Down and Out in Paris and London* and submits it to Cape. 'A Scullion's Diary' is cast in the form of a diary and is based on his Paris experiences. Resumes tramping expeditions in London.

November

1 (Sat) Thanks Max Plowman, co-editor of *Adelphi*, for sending latest issue and offers to write further book reviews. Sends revised version of 'The Spike'.

December

During the winter of 1930–31 works on thorough revision and expansion of *Down and Out in Paris and London*, recasting it as a continuous narrative and including both his Paris and London experiences.

1931

January

12 (Mon) Tells Plowman he is keen to review any books on Villon, Swift, Smollett, Poe, Twain, Zola, France or Conrad, or any on India or on 'low life in London'. Offers to send 'A Hanging'.

March

Reviews Osbert Burdett's *The Two Carlyles* in *Adelphi*.

April

'The Spike' in *Adelphi*.

June

Reviews Pearl Buck's *The Good Earth* in *Adelphi*.

July

27 (Mon) Sees an apparition in Walberswick cemetery.

August

'A Hanging' in *Adelphi*.

Types revised version of *Down and Out in Paris and London* at the home of Mabel Fierz, 1b Oakwood Road, Hampstead and submits it to Cape.

16 (Sun) Writes to Dennis Collings describing his sighting of a 'ghost' at Walberswick.

25 Begins his most extended tramping expedition at Lewis Levy's 'kip', 90–92 Westminster Bridge Road.

26 Camps in Trafalgar Square.

27 Reads *Eugénie Grandet*. Spends night in lodging house on Southwark Bridge Road.

28 Begins journey to Kentish hop fields and spends night at Bromley.

29 To Ide Hill.

30 Through Sevenoaks to Seal.

September

1 (Tues) To West Malling 'spike' (casual ward, where down and outs can obtain a night's lodging at a low price).

2–19 Hop-picking at Home Farm, Wateringbury, Kent (5 miles Southwest of Maidstone).

4 Tells Dennis Collings he hopes to make 'a saleable newspaper article' of his hop-picking experiences.

19 By train from Wateringbury to London. Spends night in lodging house in Tooley Street.

Spends remainder of September and early October working as a porter at Billingsgate fish market.

October

Cape rejects *Down and Out in Paris and London*.

8 (Thurs) Finishes his tramping adventure. During October writes an account of his hop-picking experiences at Bermondsey public library, Spa Road, SE 16, while living in lodgings at 2 Windsor Street, Paddington.

17 'Hop Picking' in *New Statesman*.

30 Asks T. S. Eliot whether Faber would publish an English translation of Jacques Roberti's *A la Belle de Nuit*.

November

Writes to Leonard Moore introducing himself and offering to submit samples of his writing.

4 (Wed) Sends copy of *A la Belle de Nuit* to Eliot and offers to translate any other French books for Faber.

In late autumn 1931 begins work on *Burmese Days*.

December

14 (Mon) Submits 'A Scullion's Diary' to Faber.

19 Becomes drunk in the hope of being sent to prison. Taken to Bethnal Green police station.

21 Released from custody. Spends night at Church Army shelter, 176 Waterloo Road. (Later writes an account of the experience under the title 'Clink'.)

At the end of month moves to cheap lodgings in Westminster Bridge Road, SE1.

1932

February

17 (Wed) Writes to T. S. Eliot reminding him about manuscript of 'A Scullion's Diary'.

19 'A Scullion's Diary' rejected by Faber.

Blair leaves manuscript with Mabel Fierz, who (unknown to Blair) recommends it to the literary agent Leonard Moore.

March

Spends several weeks staying with his sister Marjorie Blair at Bramley, Yorkshire, working on *Burmese Days*.

April

14 (Thurs) Begins full-time teaching at The Hawthorns School, 116 Church Road, Hayes, Middlesex, a small private school for boys.

26 Thanks Leonard Moore for offering to place *Down and Out in Paris and London* with a publisher but wishes it to

be issued under a pseudonym. Says he has a novel in hand [*Burmese Days*].

May

Reviews E. R. Curtius's *The Civilisation of France* in *Adelphi*.

June

9   (Thurs) Reviews Karl Adams's *The Spirit of Catholicism* in *New English Weekly*.

14 Tells Eleanor Jaques that Hayes 'is one of the most godforsaken places I have ever struck'. Tells her he has read Marlowe's *Faustus*.

30 Publishes letter in *New English Weekly* replying to criticisms of his review of Karl Adams's *The Spirit of Catholicism*.

July

1   (Fri) Tells Leonard Moore he has agreed to changes in *Down and Out in Paris and London* insisted on by Victor Gollancz.

6   Sends amended text of *Down and Out in Paris and London* to Leonard Moore and suggests 'The Lady Poverty' as a possible title.

August

Writes 'Clink' (see December 1931).

During school holidays continues to work on *Burmese Days*.

September

Tells Brenda Salkeld he has read through the draft of *Burmese Days*, 'which depresses me horribly'.

3   (Sat) 'Common Lodging Houses' in *New Statesman*.

19   Tells Eleanor Jaques he is reading Bishop Gore's *Belief in God*.

Between September and December works on a school play, 'King Charles II'.

October

19   (Wed) Tells Eleanor Jaques he reads the *Church Times* regularly and likes it more every week.

He plans to come to London on the 28th and sleep on the Embankment.

November

14   (Mon) Receives proofs of *Down and Out in Paris and London*.

15   Tells Leonard Moore he can return the corrected proofs in about a week.

18   Returns proofs of *Down and Out in Paris and London*.

19   Writes to Leonard Moore with four possible pseudonyms: P. S. Burton, Kenneth Miles, George Orwell, H. Lewis Allways. He adds 'I rather favour George Orwell.' Suggests 'The Confessions of a Dishwasher' as a possible title.

26 With Eleanor Jaques attends performance of *Macbeth* at the Old Vic, Waterloo Road, SE1.

30 Tells Eleanor Jaques he is extremely busy with school work and is looking forward to reading *Ulysses*.

December

Unemployment in Britain reaches 2.8 million, 5.6 million in Germany and 13.7 million in the US.

13 (Tues) Asks Eleanor Jaques to join him on a country walk in the Denham area on Sunday the 18th.

23 Travels to Southwold for Christmas holiday. Receives advance copies of *Down and Out in Paris and London* and writes to thank Leonard Moore.

28 To Bedfordshire to present Brenda Salkeld with her copy of *Down and Out in Paris and London*.

During the Christmas holidays continues to work on *Burmese Days*.

His reading since leaving Burma has included Richard Garnett's *The Twilight of the Gods*, Mark Twain's *Life on the Mississippi*, J. S. Haldane's *Possible Worlds*, Guy Boothby's *Dr Nikola*, Mary Sherwood's *The History of the Fairchild Family*, Robert Tressell's *The Ragged Trousered Philanthropists* and Aldous Huxley's *Brave New World*.

A George Orwell Chronology

[Part Two: George Orwell]

1933

January

9   (Mon) Gollancz published *Down and Out in Paris and London* by 'George Orwell'.

18 Resumes teaching at The Hawthorns.

30 Adolf Hitler is appointed Chancellor of Germany.

February

1   (Wed) Asks Leonard Moore for his opinion of first 100 pages of *Burmese Days*.

5   National demonstration in Hyde Park protesting against unemployment.

11 Publishes letter in *The Times* replying to criticisms of *Down and Out in Paris and London*.

18 Tells Eleanor Jaques that Leonard Moore is pleased with first section of *Burmese Days*, 'and harries me to get on with it'.

21 Hears from Leonard Moore that Harpers will publish *Down and Out in Paris and London* in the U.S.

26 Tells Eleanor Jaques he has read Charles Duff's *James Joyce and the Plain Reader* and Upton Sinclair's autobiography.

27 Hitler suspends civil liberties and freedom of the press in Germany.

March

Poem, 'Sometimes in the Middle Autumn Days', in *Adelphi*.

10 (Fri) Writes to Brenda Salkeld criticising Bernard Shaw.

25 Tells Leonard Moore he does not care to send biographical details to Harpers.

April

15 (Sat) Delivers second instalment of *Burmese Days* (a further 100 pages) to Leonard Moore.

May

Poem, 'Summer-Like', in *Adelphi*.

25 (Thurs) Writes to Eleanor Jaques suggesting a meeting.

June

Urges Brenda Salkeld to read *Ulysses*: 'It sums up better than any book I know the fearful despair that is almost normal in modern times.'

25 (Sun) George Orwell's 30th birthday.

30 Publication of American edition of *Down and Out in Paris and London* by Harpers, New York.

July

7 (Fri) Tells Eleanor Jaques he hopes to finish his novel [*Burmese Days*] by the end of this term.

20 Tells Eleanor Jaques he has completed the first draft of *Burmese Days* and has been reading the *Collected Letters* of D. H. Lawrence.

At the end of month, ceases teaching at The Hawthorns.

August

Reviews Enid Starkie's *Baudelaire* in *Adelphi*.

Spends holiday at Southwold.

September

Commences teaching at Frays College, 65 Harefield Road, Uxbridge. The school has 200 pupils and a staff of 16 teachers. George Orwell teaches French.

October

Poem, 'A Dressed Man and a Naked Man' in *Adelphi*.

14 (Sat) Germany resigns from the League of Nations.

19 Tells Leonard Moore he will complete final typescript of *Burmese Days* by the end of November.

November

26 (Sun) Tells Leonard Moore he aims to finish typing *Burmese Days* by December 2nd.

December

3? (Sun) Delivers completed typescript of *Burmese Days* to Leonard Moore.

10 Writes long letter to Brenda Salkeld discussing *Ulysses* in detail.

16? Catches pneumonia while motorcycling in torrential rain. At the end of month is admitted to Uxbridge Cottage Hospital, Harefield Road, Uxbridge, very seriously ill.

28 Tells Leonard Moore he intends to resign from teaching on health grounds: he plans to write his next novel [*A Clergyman's Daughter*] 'in six months or so'.

1934

January

During this month Gollancz and Heinemann both decline to publish *Burmese Days*.

8 (Mon) Leaves hospital and travels to 36 High Street, Southwold, where he convalesces under the care of his mother. Here he remains until October, working on *A Clergyman's Daughter*.

27 Tells Leonard Moore he is feeling much stronger and has resumed writing.

31 Travels to London to meet editor of Harpers (to discuss textual changes to *Burmese Days*).

February

2 (Fri) Suggests to Leonard Moore the idea of writing a biography of Mark Twain.

8 Tells Leonard Moore he can make necessary alterations to *Burmese Days* within three or four days.

12 Victor Gollancz tells Leonard Moore he has reconsidered *Burmese Days* and still does not wish to publish it.

March

12 (Mon) Asks Harpers to insert a note in *Burmese Days* stating 'all the characters in this story are entirely imaginary'.

April

Poem, 'On a Ruined Farm near the His Master's Voice Gramophone Factory', in *Adelphi*.

May

14 (Mon) Means-tested unemployment benefit introduced in Britain.

July

27 (Fri) Tells Brenda Salkeld he is 'struggling in the entrails of

that dreadful book' [*A Clergyman's Daughter*], and aims to finish it by October.

September

14 (Fri) Obtains his first driving licence.

October

3 (Wed) Finishes *A Clergyman's Daughter* and sends typescript to Leonard Moore.

15 (?) Leaves Southwold and takes up post as part-time assistant at Booklovers' Corner, 1 South End Road, London NW3, working five hours each day in the bookshop (until January 1936). Moves to 3 Warwick Mansions, Pond Street, Hampstead, a flat above the bookshop.

25 Publication of American edition of *Burmese Days* by Harpers, New York.

November

14 (Wed) Tells Leonard Moore he is willing to make changes to the text of *A Clergyman's Daughter* if requested by Gollancz.

19 Meets Victor Gollancz to discuss textual changes (Victor Gollancz is worried by possibility of libel).

December

17 (Mon) Submits revised text of *A Clergyman's Daughter* to Gollancz.

1935

January

22 (Tues) Leonard Moore tells him Gollancz have agreed to publish *A Clergyman's Daughter*.

February

Begins writing *Keep the Aspidistra Flying*.

1 (Fri) Gollancz asks to have another look at *Burmese Days* with a view to publication.

2 Writes to Victor Gollancz promising to send him a copy of *Burmese Days*.

16 Tells Brenda Salkeld he wants his next novel [*Keep the Aspidistra Flying*] to be 'a work of art'.

22 Meets Victor Gollancz and Harold Rubinstein (Victor Gollancz's solicitor) to discuss possible changes to *Burmese Days*.

28 Submits revised text of *Burmese Days* to Gollancz.

March

Early in March moves to 77 Parliament Hill, Hampstead, NW3. Later in the month meets Eileen O'Shaughnessy (first wife) for the first time.

6 (Wed) Sends copy of *A Clergyman's Daughter* to Brenda Salkeld, telling her 'it is tripe, except for chap 3, part 1'.

11 Publication of *A Clergyman's Daughter* by Gollancz.

May

Publication of French edition of *Down and Out in Paris and London* under the title *La Vache Enragée*, with a specially written preface by George Orwell.

June

24 (Mon) Publication of *Burmese Days* by Gollancz.

July

During this summer renews his friendship with Cyril Connolly, whom he has not met since leaving Eton.

6 (Sat) Favourable review of *Burmese Days* in *New Statesman* by Connolly.

August

Moves to a rented flat at 50 Lawford Road, Kentish Town, sharing the menage with Rayner Heppenstall and Michael Sayers. Begins reviewing fiction for *New English Weekly* (until April 1940).

September

30 (Mon) Tells Leonard Moore Gollancz has requested completion of *Keep the Aspidistra Flying* by the end of the year, aiming for publication in February 1936.

October

Proposes marriage to Eileen O'Shaughnessy, who declines until she has completed her degree course.

4   (Fri) Sees film version of Anna Karenina starring Greta Garbo.

16 Lectures on 'Confessions of a Down and Out' to South Woodford Literary Society, Essex.

26 Suggests to Leonard Moore the possibility of further lecturing engagements.

November

Poem, 'St Andrews Day, 1935', in *Adelphi*.

14 (Thurs) Reviews Henry Miller's *Tropic of Cancer* in *New English Weekly*.

1936

January

During this month accepts commission from Victor Gollancz to write a study of unemployment in the North of England [*The Road to Wigan Pier*]. At the end of the month resigns from post at Booklovers' Corner and gives up flat at 50 Lawford Road.

15 (Wed) Submits typescript of *Keep the Aspidistra Flying* to Gollancz.

23 'On Kipling's Death' in *New English Weekly*.

31 Travels to Coventry by train on the first stage of his journey north.

February

1. (Sat) Walks to Birmingham, then bus to Stourbridge, walks to Clent youth hostel.

2. Walks to Stourbridge, then bus to Wolverhampton. Walks to Penkridge, bus to Stafford. Stays at Temperance Hotel.

3. Bus to Hanley. Stays at youth hostel.

4. Walks to Macclesfield, then bus to Manchester. Stays at lodging house in Chester Street.

5. Spends day at lodging house.

6–10. Stays with Frank Meade (trade union official) at 49 Brynton Road, Longsight, Manchester.

10. Attends public meeting on unemployment, at Wigan Co-operative Hall.

11–15. In lodgings at Warrington Lane, Wigan, gathering information on housing conditions.

16–28? In lodgings above a tripe shop at 22 Darlington Street, Wigan.

17. Receives letter from Gollancz requesting further changes to *Keep the Aspidistra Flying*.

23. Goes down Cribben's coal mine, Wigan, later describing his experience in chapter 2 of *The Road to Wigan Pier*.

25. To Liverpool, where he sees corporation housing estates at St Andrew's Gardens, Brownlow Hill.

26. Returns to Wigan.

March

2 (Mon)–6 In lodgings at Wallace Road, Sheffield.

5 Reviews ten Penguin Books titles in *New English Weekly*.

7 German troops occupy demilitarised zone of Rhineland, in violation of the Versailles Treaty (later Orwell notes this event in *The Road to Wigan Pier*).

7–9 Stays with Marjorie Blair and her husband at 21 Estcourt Avenue, Headingley. Visits Haworth Parsonage, former home of the Brontë sisters.

11 To Barnsley, to arrange lodgings.

13–26 At Agnes Terrace, Barnsley, lodging with a mining family.

16 Hears Oswald Mosley (leader of the British Union of Fascists) speak at Barnsley Public Hall.

17 Offers to review Alec Brown's *The Fate of the Middle Classes* for *Adelphi*.

17 Tells Jack Common he thinks war will not break out this year.

19 Goes down Wentworth pit.

21 Goes down Grimethorpe pit.

23 At Mapplewell: 'Houses about the worst I have seen.'

26 To Leeds.

30 Returns to London.

April

1   (Wed) Visits Eileen O'Shaughnessy.

2   Moves to a village shop at The Stores, Wallington, Hertfordshire.

16 Tells Jack Common he has decided to re-open the village shop.

20 Tells Richard Rees he is 'all set' to begin his new book [*The Road to Wigan Pier*].

20 Publication of *Keep the Aspidistra Flying* by Gollancz.

May

Begins writing *The Road to Wigan Pier*.

Left Book Club founded by Victor Gollancz.

11 (Mon) Opens the shop, selling groceries and sweets.

27 Submits proposal to write 'Shooting an Elephant' to *New Writing*.

June

8   (Mon) Thanks Anthony Powell for sending his volume of poetry, *Caledonia*.

9   Marries Eileen O'Shaughnessy at Wallington parish church.

12 Sends 'Shooting an Elephant' to *New Writing*.

July

18 (Sat) Spanish Civil War begins with fighting between Republican (socialist) forces and Nationalist (anti-socialist) forces.

23 Reviews Cyril Connolly's *The Rock Pool* and Conrad's *Almayer's Folly* in *New English Weekly*.

August

Trials of prominent Communists opposed to Stalin's regime begin in Moscow. All plead guilty to their alleged crimes.

4 (Wed) Lectures on 'An Outsider sees the Depressed Areas' at the *Adelphi* summer school at Langham, Essex.

17 Publication of American edition of *A Clergyman's Daughter* by Harpers, New York.

26 Thanks Henry Miller for sending *Black Spring*.

September

'Shooting an Elephant' in *New Writing*.

24 (Fri) Reviews Henry Miller's *Black Spring*, E. M. Forster's *A Passage to India*, and Richard Aldington's *Death of a Hero* in *New English Weekly*.

October

Early in the month finishes rough draft of *The Road to Wigan Pier*. Begins work on revision.

November

'Bookshop Memories' in *Fortnightly*.

At about this time decides to go to Spain as soon as *The Road to Wigan Pier* is finished.

12 (Fri) 'In Defence of the Novel' in *New English Weekly*.

December

Poem, 'A Happy Vicar', in *Adelphi*.

8 (Tues) Issued with a passport.

11 Tells Leonard Moore to deal with Eileen O'Shaughnessy on all literary matters during his absence in Spain.

15 Sends manuscript of *The Road to Wigan Pier* to Leonard Moore.

19 Victor Gollancz suggests an urgent meeting to discuss manuscript.

21 Meets Victor Gollancz to discuss publication of *The Road to Wigan Pier*.

23 Leaves England en route for Spain.

24 Visits Paris to collect Spanish travel documents. Calls on Henry Miller.

26 Arrives in Barcelona.

30 Enlists in the militia of the POUM (Workers' Party of Marxist Unification).

1937

January

Spends first week in January at the Lenin Barracks, Barcelona.

7? (Thurs) To the front line at Alcubierre, where he remains until 2 February.

February

2 (Tues) Transfers, as a corporal, to the Independent Labour Party contingent at Monte Trazo, a few miles from Alcubierre on the Aragon front.

15 Eileen O'Shaughnessy leaves England en route for Spain (to work in the Barcelona office of the ILP).

15? Moves to the outskirts of Huesca.

19 Bob Edwards, leader of the ILP contingent, praises Orwell's heroism.

March

8 (Mon) Publication of *The Road to Wigan Pier*.

13–14 Eileen O'Shaughnessy spends two days at the front.

At the end of the month, Orwell spends ten days in hospital at Monflorite, a short distance behind the front, with an infected hand wound.

April

At the end of the month Orwell is granted leave and

travels to Barcelona. He applies for his discharge, intending to join the International Brigade.

30   (Fri) 'Night Attack on the Aragon Front' in *New Leader*.

May

3   (Mon)–7 Rioting and street fighting in Barcelona. Orwell spends much time on guard duty on the roof of the Poliorama cinema, guarding the POUM Headquarters opposite.

9   Thanks Victor Gollancz for writing the introduction for *The Road to Wigan Pier*.

10   Returns to the front as a second lieutenant.

20   Shot in the throat by a Fascist sniper. He is taken to hospital at Monflorite, then to another hospital at Sietamo.

22?   To hospital at Lerida.

29   Moves to a sanatorium at Mount Tibidabo, near Barcelona, where he remains for two weeks.

June

8   (Tues) Tells Cyril Connolly that 'at last [I] really believe in Socialism, which I never did before.'

15   Returns to the front to collect his discharge papers. Remains at the front until the 20th.

16   Spanish Government declares the POUM illegal.

20–23   In hiding in Barcelona.

23 Together with Eileen O'Shaughnessy, escapes from Barcelona by train. Spends a few days resting at Banyuls sur Mer, a fishing town on the French coast. Returns to London at the end of June.

July

Early in July returns to The Stores, Wallington. Begins writing *Homage to Catalonia*.

5 (Mon) Victor Gollancz declines to publish *Homage to Catalonia* on the grounds that it would 'harm the fight against fascism'.

6 Fredric Warburg offers to publish *Homage to Catalonia*.

8 Tells Leonard Moore that Victor Gollancz will not publish the book.

29 'Spilling the Spanish Beans' in *New English Weekly* (first instalment).

31 Reviews Franz Borkenau's *The Spanish Cockpit* in *Time and Tide*.

August

'Eye-Witness in Barcelona' in *Controversy*.

5 (Thurs) Speaks on his Spanish Civil War experiences at the ILP Summer School at Letchworth.

16 Tells Geoffrey Gorer 'You cannot conceive the awfulness of the things that are happening in Spain.'

September

1 (Wed) Signs contract with Secker and Warburg for publication of *Homage to Catalonia*.

2 'Spilling the Spanish Beans' in *New English Weekly* (final instalment).

October

9 (Sat) Reviews Mary Low's *Red Spanish Notebook* in *Time and Tide*.

November

5 (Fri) Air Raid Precautions Bill introduced in House of Commons.

December

Early in the month completes first draft of *Homage to Catalonia*.

1 (Wed) Accepts Cyril Connolly's invitation to lunch on the 3rd.

3 Lunches with Cyril Connolly and Stephen Spender.

6 Tells Leonard Moore he has an idea for a new novel to be entitled *Coming Up for Air*.

11 Reviews Mairin Mitchell's *Storm over Spain*, Arnold Lunn's *Spanish Rehearsal* and Allison Peers's *Catalonia Infelix* in *Time and Tide*.

1938

January

Completes final text of *Homage to Catalonia*.

February

During this month receives an invitation from the *Pioneer* newspaper to take up a journalistic appointment in Lucknow, India.

5 (Sat) Reviews Arthur Koestler's *Spanish Testament* in *Time and Tide*.

9 Writes to Raymond Mortimer (literary editor of *New Statesman*) apropos the *New Statesman*'s refusal to publish his review of *The Spanish Cockpit*.

12 Writes to A. H. Joyce at the India Office summarising his career and seeking Joyce's views on his proposed appointment in India.

20 Anthony Eden, British Foreign Secretary, resigns in protest at Chamberlain's policy of appeasement.

March

8 (Tues) Falls ill with tubercular lesion.

9 Begins writing a diary of domestic matters (until April 1940).

9 Reviews Maurice Collis's *Trials in Burma* in *The Listener*.

11 German troops enter Austria, which is declared part of the German Reich.

12 Reviews Galsworthy's *Glimpses and Reflections* in *New Statesman*.

14 Asks Cyril Connolly to send a copy of his forthcoming book *Enemies of Promise*.

15 Admitted to Preston Hall Sanatorium, Aylesford, Kent, suffering from haemorrhages and suspected tuberculosis. George Orwell remains at the sanatorium for six months, instructed not to work apart from letters, crossword puzzles, and occasional book reviews.

April

2 (Sat) Writes to Stephen Spender hoping he will read *Homage to Catalonia*.

15 Thanks Stephen Spender for sending his play *Trial of a Judge*.

18 Thanks Geoffrey Gorer for his favourable review of *Homage to Catalonia* in *Time and Tide*.

20 Thanks Jack Common for sending *Seven Shifts*, which he has read with pleasure.

25 Publication of *Homage to Catalonia* in an edition of 1,500 copies.

27 Tells Cyril Connolly that if the Spanish Civil War is lost, another world war will become inevitable.

May

26 (Thurs) Publishes letter in *New English Weekly* urging the need for an effective anti-war movement in Britain.

30 Eileen O'Shaughnessy tells Leonard Moore that the idea for a new novel [*Coming Up for Air*] 'seethes in his head and he is very anxious to get on with it'.

June

9 (Thurs) Reviews Eugene Lyons's *Assignment in Utopia* in *New English Weekly*.

16 Reviews Jack Common's *The Freedom of the Streets* in *New English Weekly*.

24 'Why I Joined the Independent Labour Party' in *New Leader*.

27 Tells C. D. Abbott (of the State University of New York at Buffalo) 'I don't really write verse.'

July

George Orwell is advised to spend the coming winter in a warm climate. The novelist L. H. Myers makes Orwell an anonymous loan of £300 to enable him and Eileen O'Shaughnessy to go abroad.

5 (Tues) Writes to Jack Common offering the cottage at Wallington rent-free for 6 months, in return for looking after the animals (fowls and goats).

8 Reviews Frank Jellinek's *The Civil War in Spain* in *New Leader*.

8 Tells Cyril Connolly he keeps toying with the idea of starting his new novel [*Coming Up for Air*], and feels the rest in the sanatorium has done him good.

21 Reviews the Duchess of Atholl's *Searchlight on Spain* in *New English Weekly*.

August

8   (Mon) Tells Ida Blair that he and his wife will visit Southwold before going abroad.

25 Asks Frank Westrope (of Booklovers' Corner) to send maps of Morocco together with an Arabic phrase book and dictionary.

September

Begins writing *Coming Up for Air*.

1   (Thurs) Leaves sanatorium.

2   Sails from Tilbury to Gibraltar en route for Morocco on the S. S. *Stratheden*, a P & O liner.

14 Arrives in Marrakesh, having travelled by train from Tangier. He and Eileen O'Shaughnessy remain in Marrakesh for one month, staying at the home of Madame Vellat, rue Edmond Doutte, Medinah.

22 Reviews Franz Borkenau's *The Communist International* in *New English Weekly*.

26 Tells Jack Common he does not plan to return to England until the spring.

29 At the Munich Conference, Chamberlain, Hitler, Mussolini and Daladier agree to the dismemberment of Czechoslovakia. Germany becomes the dominant power in Europe.

October

1   (Sat) Germany occupies Sudetenland.

12 Tells Jack Common he does not intend to give up the cottage at Wallington.

15 Moves to Villa Simont, Sidahan, Route de Casablanca, Marrakesh.

26 Writes to John Sceats, an insurance agent, seeking background detail for *Coming Up for Air*.

November

24 (Thurs) Tells John Sceats 'I've decided to count 1938 as a blank year and sort of cross it off the calendar.' He feels he could write a good novel if he had five years peace and quiet.

29 Eileen O'Shaughnessy asks Frank Westrope (of Booklovers' Corner) to send some Dickens: 'We are desperate for something to read, something *long*.'

December

14 (Wed) Asks Cyril Connolly to send *Enemies of Promise* as he cannot obtain English books in Morocco.

20 Asks Leonard Moore to send a copy of *Homage to Catalonia* to Frank Jellinek.

26 Tells Jack Common he aims to complete his novel [*Coming Up for Air*] by the beginning of April. He is contemplating writing 'an enormous novel in several volumes' but needs several years of peace.

1939

January

Finishes rough draft of *Coming Up for Air*.

- 4 (Wed) Agrees to sign manifesto calling for the formation of an International Federation of Independent Revolutionary Art.

- 12 Reviews N. de Basily's *Russia under Soviet Rule* in *New English Weekly*.

- 13 Publishes letter in *New Leader* apologising for having misrepresented the writer Frank Jellinek.

- 20 Tells Geoffrey Gorer he has an idea for a novel 'about the size of *War and Peace*'.

- 20? Leaves Marrakesh for a week's holiday at Taddert in the Atlas mountains.

- 27 Returns to Marrakesh, where he is ill for three weeks.

March

- 5 (Sun) Writes to Herbert Read agreeing to contribute to the anarchist paper *Revolt*.

- 15 German troops occupy remainder of Czechoslovakia.

- 26 Sails to Britain from Casablanca. During the journey types the manuscript of *Coming Up for Air*.

- 28 Spanish Civil War ends as Madrid surrenders to General Franco.

30 Arrives in Britain. Delivers *Coming Up for Air* to Gollancz, then travels to Southwold, where his father is seriously ill.

April

11 (Tues) Arrives home in Wallington from Southwold.

May

Spends first three weeks in May visiting Eileen O'Shaughnessy's brother Laurence at 24 Crooms Hill, Greenwich.

24 (Wed) Returns to Wallington, where he begins work on the essay 'Charles Dickens'.

June

12 (Mon) Publication of *Coming Up for Air* in an edition of 2,000 copies. A reprint of 1,000 copies is issued in the same month.

19 Sends chapters 7–10 of *Homage to Catalonia* to Yvonne Davet for a French translation. Promises to send remainder in a few days.

24 To Southwold to be with his father, who is terminally ill.

28 Death of Richard Walmesley Blair (father).

July

'Not Counting Niggers' in *Adelphi*.

Finishes writing 'Charles Dickens'.

1? (Sat) Returns to Wallington.

14 Tells Leonard Moore he is contemplating a long novel 'which will have to be published in three parts'. (George Orwell later gives the title *The Quick and the Dead* to this project.)

27 Reviews F. C. Green's *Stendhal* in *New English Weekly*.

August

23 (Wed) Germany and USSR sign non-aggression pact. British Government warns Hitler that Britain will stand by Poland.

24–31 Stays with L. H. Myers at Ringwood, Hampshire.

September

'Democracy in the British Army' in *Left Forum*.

Eileen O'Shaughnessy moves to Crooms Hill, Greenwich, to live with her brother's wife.

She takes up a post in the Censorship Department, joining George Orwell at Wallington at weekends.

1 (Fri) Germany invades Poland.

3 Britain declares war on Germany. Second World War begins.

December

Finishes writing *Inside the Whale*.

1940

January

8 (Mon) Tells Victor Gollancz he cannot lend his copy of *Tropic of Cancer* as it has been seized by the police.

8 Food rationing begins in Britain.

10 Tells Geoffrey Gorer he has completely failed to serve HM Government in any capacity.

20 Reviews S. Casado's *The Last Days of Madrid* in *Time and Tide*.

25 Tells Leonard Moore he has been reading Hitler's *Mein Kampf* 'with some interest'.

30 To 24 Crooms Hill, Greenwich, where he remains for six weeks (part of the time ill with influenza).

February

'The Lessons of War' in *Horizon*.

March

'Boys' Weeklies' in *Horizon*.

11 (Mon) Publication of *Inside the Whale* (containing 'Charles Dickens', 'Boys' Weeklies' and 'Inside the Whale').

13 Returns home to Wallington.

21 Reviews Hitler's *Mein Kampf* in *New English Weekly*.

29 Reviews *The Memoirs of Sergeant Bourgogne* in *Tribune* (his first contribution to *Tribune*).

30 'Notes on the Way' in *Time and Tide*.

April

3 (Wed) Tells Geoffrey Gorer he is trying hard to join a Government training centre and learn machine draughtsmanship.

6 'Notes on the Way' in *Time and Tide*.

11 Writes to Humphry House commenting in detail on the *Manifesto of the Common Man* drawn up by Sir Richard Acland.

17 Writes 'Autobiographical Note' for inclusion in *Twentieth Century Authors* (New York, Wilson, 1942).

25 'The Limit to Pessimism' in *New English Weekly*.

29 Last entry in domestic diary.

May

Leaves Wallington and moves (with Eileen O'Shaughnessy) to 18 Dorset Chambers, Chagford Street, near Regent's Park.

4 (Sat) Reviews Borkenau's *The Totalitarian Enemy* in *Time and Tide*.

10 Germany invades Holland, Luxembourg and Belgium. Winston Churchill becomes Prime Minister. Formation of the Local Defence Volunteers (later renamed the Home Guard).

18 Begins regular weekly theatre criticism for *Time and Tide*.

28 Begins writing 'War-Time Diary' (until November 1942).

29 Dunkirk evacuation begins.

31 Sees Denis Ogden's play *The Peaceful Inn*.

June

Early in June, Eileen O'Shaughnessy's brother Laurence is killed at Dunkirk.

3   (Mon) Dunkirk evacuation ends.

8   *The Times* announces death of Laurence O'Shaughnessy.

12 Joins the Home Guard. Becomes a sergeant in C Company of the 5th County of London Battalion (St John's Wood), organising regular drills at the Drill Hall, Allitsen Road, London, NW8, commanding a platoon of 60 men.

20 Notes in his diary: 'Thinking always of my islands in the Hebrides.'

21 Reviews Wells's *Film Stories* in *Tribune*.

22 Publishes letter in *Time and Tide* urging arming the civilian population.

28 Rejected for military service on medical grounds.

30 Attends Home Guard parade in Regent's Park.

July

6   (Sat) Tells John Lehmann 'I just can't write with this kind of thing [the war] going on.'

12 'Prophecies of Fascism' in *Tribune*.

16 Hitler orders the German armed forces to prepare for an invasion of England.

August

Begins writing *The Lion and the Unicorn*.

3 (Sat) Reviews Bernard Shaw's *The Devil's Disciple* in *Time and Tide*.

13–14 At Wallington for 'two glorious days'.

17 'Charles Reade' in *New Statesman*.

23 Reviews George and Weedon Grossmith's *The Diary of a Nobody* in *Tribune*.

23 Receives his Home Guard uniform.

23 German bombing raid on London begins the 'Blitz'.

September

'My Country Right or Left' in *Folios of New Writing*.

Reviews Sacheverell Sitwell's *Poltergeists* in *Horizon*.

October

Finishes writing *The Lion and the Unicorn*.

15 (Tues) At Wallington, having been ill with blood poisoning.

November

27 (Wed) Lunches with Pierre Comert, editor of *France*.

December

'The Ruling Class' in *Horizon*.

6 (Fri) 'The Proletarian Writer', a discussion between George Orwell and Desmond Hawkins, broadcast on BBC Home Service.

7 Reviews Nevil Shute's *Landfall* in *New Statesman*.

19 'The Proletarian Writer' in *The Listener*.

21 Reviews Chaplin's film *The Great Dictator* in *Time and Tide*.

1941

January

3 (Fri) Writes 'London Letter' for the American literary journal *Partisan Review* (the first of 15 London Letters George Orwell contributes during 1941–46). The first is published in the March 1941 issue.

February

19 (Wed) Publication of *The Lion and the Unicorn*.

March

3 (Mon) Publication of *The Betrayal of the Left*, containing

two chapters by Orwell, 'Fascism and Democracy' and 'Patriots and Revolutionaries'.

4 At Wallington.

22 Attends a Home Guard church parade to mark the national day of prayer.

April

At the beginning of the month, Orwell and his wife move to a flat at 111 Langford Court, Abbey Road, St John's Wood.

8 (Tues) Reads *The Battle of Britain*, published by the Ministry of Information.

12 Registers (for national identification purposes) together with all other males in the district born in the same year. Notes in his diary how rapidly the working classes age.

15 Writes second 'London Letter' for *Partisan Review* (published July).

21–22 At Wallington, sowing potatoes.

May

10 (Sat) Rudolf Hess, prominent Nazi, flies to Britain, allegedly bearing peace proposals.

13 Orwell notes in his diary that Hess's arrival is 'completely mysterious'.

17 Reviews film version of H. G. Wells's *Kipps* in *Time and Tide*.

23 Lectures on 'Literature and Totalitarianism' to Oxford University English Club.

24 Reviews Stephen Spender's *The Backward Son* in *Tribune*.

29 'The Frontiers of Art and Propaganda' in *The Listener*.

June

3 (Tues) Passes medical examination at Willesden, grade four (i.e. the lowest grade).

5 'Tolstoy and Shakespeare' in *The Listener*.

12 'The Meaning of a Poem' in *The Listener*.

19 'Literature and Totalitarianism' in *The Listener*.

20 Sends letter of condolence to Dorothy Plowman on the death of her husband Max.

22 Germany invades Russia.

23 Welcomes Churchill's speech on German invasion.

August

'Wells, Hitler and the World State' in *Horizon*.

17 (Sun) Writes third 'London Letter' for *Partisan Review* (published November).

18 Joins the staff of the British Broadcasting Corporation as a Talks Assistant, later becoming a Talks Producer, in the Indian Section of its Eastern Service. Orwell works from offices at 200 Oxford Street, London W1 (until November 1943).

30 H. G. Wells dines at the Orwells'.

October

'No, Not One' in *Adelphi*.

'Why Not War Writers? A Manifesto' in *Horizon*.

21 (Tues) Broadcast talk: 'From Colliery to Kitchen'.

November

22 (Sat) Lectures to the Fabian Society on 'Culture and Democracy'.

December

20 (Sat) Begins regular weekly news talks on the progress of the war (until March 1943). These are *written* by Orwell but not usually broadcast by him.

1942

January

1 (Thurs) Writes 'London Letter' for *Partisan Review* (published March).

20 Gives broadcast talk, 'Money and Guns'.

22 Gives broadcast talk, 'British Rations and the Submarine War'.

29 Gives broadcast talk, 'The Meaning of Sabotage'.

February

'The Art of Donald McGill' in *Horizon*.

'Rudyard Kipling' in *Horizon*.

March

- 8 (Sun) 'Mood of the Moment' in *Observer*, the first of many articles and reviews for this paper.
- 10 Gives broadcast talk, 'The Rediscovery of Europe', on BBC Eastern Service.
- 14 Resumes War Diary after a gap of six months.
- 19 'The Rediscovery of Europe' in *The Listener*.

April

Eileen O'Shaughnessy begins working for the Ministry of Food, preparing the 'Kitchen Front' broadcast talks.

- 19 (Sun) 'Mood of the Moment' in *Observer*.
- 29 To the House of Commons to hear the debate on Indian independence.

May

- 8 (Fri) Writes 'London Letter' for *Partisan Review*, under the title 'The British Crisis' (published July).
- 10 Reviews Edmund Wilson's *The Wound and the Bow* in *Observer*.

13 Meets Sir Stafford Cripps, Leader of the House of Commons, to discuss the Indian situation.

June

At about this time Orwell moves to 10a Mortimer Crescent, Maida Vale, London.

 2 (Tues) Spends evening with Sir Stafford Cripps. Also present are William Empson, Jack Common, Norman Cameron and Guy Burgess.

11 Notes in his diary the German announcement that the Czech village of Lidice is to be razed to the ground. Makes list of atrocities perpetrated by both sides.

July

Reviews Mulk Raj Anand's *The Sword and the Sickle* in *Horizon*.

 1 (Wed)–10 on holiday at Callow End, Worcestershire, staying on a farm.

25–26 On Home Guard manœuvres.

August

11 (Tues) First instalment of 'Voice', a poetry magazine in five parts edited and presented by Orwell for radio transmission.

29 Writes 'London Letter' for *Partisan Review* (published November).

September

'Pacifism and the War' in *Partisan Review*.

8   (Tues) Second instalment of 'Voice'.

10   Lectures at Morley College, Lambeth.

21   Meets B. H. Liddell Hart for the first time.

October

Reviews T. S. Eliot's 'Burnt Norton', 'East Coker' and 'The Dry Salvages' in *Poetry London*.

During this autumn writes 'Looking Back on the Spanish War.'

6   (Tues) Third instalment of 'Voice'.

9   'Story by Five Authors' broadcast on BBC (Part One by Orwell).

12   Writes letter to *The Times* on the treatment of German prisoners of war.

15   Sends memorandum to Eastern Service Director, BBC, agreeing to write and broadcast weekly news reviews to India under the name 'George Orwell'.

November

2   (Mon) Broadcast talk, 'Jonathan Swift, an Imaginary Interview'.

3   Fourth instalment of 'Voice'.

21 Reviews B. H. Liddell Hart's *The British Way in Warfare* in *New Statesman*.

December

2 (Wed) Writes to George Woodcock defending his role within the BBC.

21 Writes to Bernard Shaw requesting permission to quote a passage from *Arms and the Man* for a broadcast to India.

29 Final instalment of poetry magazine 'Voice'.

1943

January

'W. B. Yeats' in *Horizon*.

3 (Sun) Writes 'Letter from England' to *Partisan Review* (published March).

8 Broadcast talk, 'Edmund Blunden'.

9 'Pamphlet Literature' in *New Statesman*.

12 T. S. Eliot dines at the Orwells'.

21 Reviews Mass Observation's *The Pub and the People* in *The Listener*.

22 Broadcast talk, 'Bernard Shaw'.

March

5 (Fri) Broadcast talk, 'Jack London'.

13 The last of his weekly news commentaries on BBC radio.

19 Death of Ida Blair in New End Hospital, Hampstead. Orwell is present at the death.

April

2 (Fri) 'Not Enough Money: A Sketch of George Gissing' in *Tribune*.

May

9 (Sun) 'Three Years of the Home Guard: A Unique Symbol of Stability' in *Observer*.

27 Reviews D. W. Brogan's *The English People*.

June

4 (Fri) 'Literature and the Left' in *Tribune*.

13 Broadcast talk, 'English Poetry since 1900'.

18 'As One Non-Combatant to Another' in *Tribune*.

25 Orwell's 40th birthday.

July

11 (Sun) Thanks Alex Comfort for sending a copy of the poetry anthology *New Road*.

August

11 (Wed) 'Crainquebille' by Anatole France, adapted for radio by George Orwell.

September

Reviews Lionel Fielden's *Beggar my Neighbour* in *Horizon*.

9 (Thurs) 'The Fox' by Ignazio Silone, adapted for radio by George Orwell.

23 Collins commission Orwell to write *The English People*.

24 Resigns from BBC (his resignation takes effect on 24 November).

October

6 (Wed) 'A Slip under the Microscope' by H. G. Wells, adapted for radio by George Orwell.

17 'Macbeth', a radio commentary by George Orwell.

22 'Who are the War Criminals?' in *Tribune*.

22 Pronounced medically unfit for service overseas.

November

Appointed literary editor of *Tribune*, working from offices at 222 Strand, London WC2.

Begins writing *Animal Farm*.

17 (Wed) 'The Detective Story' in *Fontaine*.

18 Publication of *Talking to India*, edited and introduced by George Orwell.

18 'The Emperor's New Clothes' by Hans Andersen, adapted for radio by George Orwell.

21 'Lady Windermere's Fan', a radio commentary by George Orwell.

23 Resigns from Home Guard.

24 Effective date of resignation from BBC.

26 'Mark Twain – The Licensed Jester' in *Tribune*.

December

Begins regular book reviewing for the *Observer*.

2 (Thurs) Gives broadcast talk: 'What is the Wigan Pier?'

3 'As I Please' in *Tribune* (his first contribution under this title). The column appears every week until February 1945.

9 Begins book reviewing for *Manchester Evening News* under the title 'Life, People and Books', appearing each alternate week (until November 1946).

9 Tells Philip Rahv he has another book in hand [*Animal Farm*], which he hopes to finish in a few months.

19 Reviews W. H. Davies's *Collected Poems* in *Observer*.

24 'Can Socialists Be Happy?' in *Tribune*.

29 Joins National Union of Journalists.

1944

January

15 (Sat) Writes 'London Letter' for *Partisan Review* (published March).

20 Reviews James Burnham's *The Machiavellians* in *Manchester Evening News*.

February

Finishes writing *Animal Farm*.

13 (Sun) 'A Hundred Up' in *Observer*.

17 Thanks Gleb Struve for sending *25 Years of Soviet Russian Literature* and in particular for drawing his attention to Zamyatin's *We*.

27 Reviews Alfred Noyes's *The Edge of the Abyss* in *Observer*.

March

2 (Thus) Reviews Harry Levin's *James Joyce* in *Manchester Evening News*.

12 Reviews A. P. Wavell's *Other Men's Flowers* in *Observer*.

19 Asks Victor Gollancz if he wishes to see the manuscript of *Animal Farm* but warns him it is 'anti-Stalin'.

23 Reviews *The Way of a Countryman* by Sir W. Beach Thomas in *Manchester Evening News*.

23 Victor Gollancz asks to see the manuscript of *Animal Farm*.

25   Sends manuscript to Victor Gollancz.

April

Writes 'Propaganda and Demotic Speech' (published in *Persuasion*, Summer 1944).

4   (Tues) *Animal Farm* rejected by Gollancz.

9   Reviews F. A. Hayek's *The Road to Serfdom* and K. Zilliacus's *The Mirror of the Past* in *Observer*.

17   Writes 'London Letter' for *Partisan Review* (published Summer 1944).

20   Reviews Edmund Blunden's *Cricket Country* in *Manchester Evening News*.

May

Finishes writing *The English People*.

14   (Sun) Birth of Orwell's adopted son (see entry for June).

21   Reviews H. G. Wells's *'42 to '44: A Contemporary Memoir* in *Observer*.

June

Writes 'Benefit of Clergy: Some Notes on Salvador Dali'.

Orwell and his wife adopt a baby boy, whom they name Richard Horatio Blair.

11   (Sun) Meets Graham Greene for the first time.

13 First flying bomb (V1) dropped on London. Orwell notes that the weapon 'is an exceptionally unpleasant thing because, unlike most other projectiles, it gives you time to think.'

19 Cape rejects *Animal Farm*.

28 Sends manuscript of *Animal Farm* to Faber and Faber.

28 His flat at 10a Mortimer Crescent is bombed. Orwell and his wife move temporarily to 106 George Street, off Baker Street.

July

Reads Arthur Koestler's *The Gladiators*.

13 (Thurs) Faber rejects *Animal Farm*.

16 'The Eight Years of War: Spanish Memories' in *Observer*.

18 Tells Leonard Moore that Warburg has asked to see *Animal Farm*.

21 Asks Rayner Heppenstall to write a horoscope of Richard Horatio Blair.

24 Writes 'London Letter' for *Partisan Review* (published Fall 1944).

August

11 (Fri) Apologises to John Middleton Murry for having misrepresented Murry's attitude to the USSR.

29 Fredric Warburg agrees to publish *Animal Farm* as soon as supplies of paper are adequate.

September

Writes essay, 'Arthur Koestler'.

During September visits the island of Jura for the first time.

3   (Sun) 'Back to the Land' in *Observer*.

7   'How Long is a Short Story?' in *Manchester Evening News*.

8   First rocket bomb (V2) lands in Britain. Orwell notes later 'What depresses me most about these things is the way they set people talking about the next war.'

22 'Tobias Smollett: Scotland's Best Novelist' in *Tribune*.

October

Moves to 27b Canonbury Square, Islington.

Reads C. S. Lewis's *Beyond Personality*.

Begins planning contents of *Critical Essays*.

'Raffles and Miss Blandish' in *Horizon*.

15 (Sun) 'Home Guard: Lessons for the Future' in *Observer*.

November

2   (Thurs) Reviews Trollope's *The Warden* and George Eliot's *Silas Marner* in *Manchester Evening News*.

10 Reviews Oliver Goldsmith's *The Vicar of Wakefield* in *Tribune*.

30 'A Controversy: Orwell-Agate' in *Manchester Evening News*.

December

Writes 'London Letter' to *Partisan Review* (published Winter 1944).

21 (Thurs) 'A Controversy: Orwell-Agate' continued in *Manchester Evening News*.

22 'Oysters and Brown Stout' in *Tribune*.

31 'Poet in Darkness' [Baudelaire] in *Observer*.

1945

January

5 (Fri) 'Books and the People: A New Year Message' in *Tribune*.

14 Reviews Cyril Connolly's *The Unquiet Grave* in *Observer*.

22 Sends manuscript of *Critical Essays* to Leonard Moore.

February

Resigns as literary editor of *Tribune*.

Accepts invitation from *Observer* to visit France and Germany as a war correspondent.

March

'Poetry and the Microphone' in *New Saxon Pamphlets*.

15 (Thurs) To Paris as a war correspondent, staying at the Hotel Scribe, rue Scribe.

20   'The French Believe We Have Had a Revolution' in *Manchester Evening News*.

22   Eileen O'Shaughnessy tells him she has to undergo a hysterectomy operation and will enter hospital in Newcastle.

24? To Cologne, where he falls ill.

29   Death of Eileen O'Shaughnessy while under an anaesthetic, aged 39.

30   Hears of Eileen O'Shaughnessy's death and leaves at once for Britain.

31   Prepares 'Notes for my Literary Executor'.

April

'Antisemitism in Britain' in *Contemporary Jewish Record*.

8   (Sun) Returns to Paris, where he spends one week at the Hotel Scribe, then two weeks in south Germany (based in Nuremberg), then Stuttgart.

8   'The Future of a Ruined Germany' in *Observer*.

30   Death of Adolf Hitler.

May

Spends one more week in Paris, then travels to Austria before returning to England. Sends despatches to *Observer* and *Manchester Evening News*.

4   (Fri) 'Now Germany Faces Hunger' in *Manchester Evening News*.

4 Publishes letter in *Tribune* protesting against the imprisonment of the editors of *War Commentary*.

8 Germany surrenders to Allied forces; end of the war in Europe.

11 Tells Lydia Jackson he wishes to retain the Wallington cottage for occasional weekend visits.

24 Arrives back in London.

27 'Obstacles to Joint Rule in Germany' in *Observer*.

June

Begins writing an early version of *Nineteen Eighty-Four*.

5 (Tues) Writes 'London Letter' for *Partisan Review* (published Summer 1945).

8 Gives broadcast talk: '*Erewhon* by Samuel Butler'.

13 Tells Warburg he will send the 'blurb' for *Animal Farm* as soon as possible.

15 Gives broadcast talk: '*The Way of all Flesh* by Samuel Butler'.

24 Reviews Conrad's *The Nigger of the Narcissus*, *Typhoon*, *The Shadow Line* and *Within the Tides* in *Observer*.

In late June and early July reports on the General Election for the *Observer*.

July

'In Defence of P. G. Wodehouse' in *Windmill*.

3 (Tues) Tells Leonard Moore he has recently started a new novel [an early version of *Nineteen Eighty-Four*].

3 Signs contract to write four long articles for the new journal *Polemic*.

5 'Authors Deserve a New Deal' in *Manchester Evening News*.

21 'Personal Notes on Scientifiction' in *Leader Magazine*.

26 Labour wins British General Election with large majority.

28 'Funny, But Not Vulgar' in *Leader*.

August

Accepts vice-chairmanship of Freedom Defence Committee.

6 (Mon) Atomic bomb dropped on Hiroshima.

9 Atomic bomb dropped on Nagasaki.

14 Japan surrenders; end of the Second World War.

15 Writes 'London Letter' for *Partisan Review* (published Fall 1945).

17 Publication of *Animal Farm* in an edition of 4,500 copies.

18 Tells Herbert Read he is trying to buy a cottage on the island of Jura.

September

2 (Sun) 'Charles the Great' [Charles Dickens] in *Observer*.

10–22 Visits Jura in the Scottish Hebrides.

October

'Notes on Nationalism' in *Polemic*.

7 (Sun) Reviews Dostoevsky's *The Brothers Karamazov* and *Crime and Punishment* in *Observer*.

14 'Profile of Aneurin Bevan' in *Observer*.

19 'You and the Atom Bomb' in *Tribune*.

26 'What is Science?' in *Tribune*.

28 Reviews Sean O'Casey's *Drums under the Windows* in *Observer*.

November

Writes Introduction to *Love of Life and Other Stories* by Jack London.

'Catastrophic Gradualism' in *Common Wealth Review*.

'The British General Election' in *Commentary*.

2 (Fri) 'Good Bad Books' in *Tribune*.

8 Reviews H. G. Wells's *Mind at the End of its Tether* in *Manchester Evening News*.

9 'Revenge is Sour' in *Tribune*.

15 Declines to speak at a meeting of the League of European Freedom.

15 'My Dear Watson' in *Manchester Evening News*.

16 Reviews D. H. Lawrence's *The Prussian Officer and Other Stories* in *Tribune*.

18   Reviews R. L. Stevenson's *Novels and Stories* in *Observer*.

23   'Through a Glass Rosily' in *Tribune*.

December

Writes Introduction to *The Position of Peggy Harper* by Leonard Merrick. At the end of 1945 meets Sonia Brownell for the first time.

1   (Sat) 'Bare Christmas for the Children' in *Evening Standard*.

7   'Freedom of the Park' in *Tribune*.

8   'The Case for the Open Fire' in *Evening Standard*.

14 'The Sporting Spirit' in *Tribune*.

15 'In Defence of English Cooking' in *Evening Standard*.

21 'Nonsense Poetry' in *Tribune*.

22 'Banish this Uniform' in *Evening Standard*.

25 Orwell and his adopted son Richard spend Christmas with Arthur Koestler and his wife at their home in North Wales.

28 'Old George's Almanac by Crystal Gazer Orwell' in *Tribune*.

Records in his 'Payment Notebook' that he has written 109,850 words during 1945; 10,000 more than in 1944.

1946

January

'The Prevention of Literature' in *Polemic*.

4 (Fri) Reviews Zamyatin's *We* in *Tribune*.

5 'Just Junk' in *Evening Standard*.

11 'Pleasure Spots' in *Tribune*.

12 'A Nice Cup of Tea' in *Evening Standard*.

13 Reviews *Collected Stories of Katherine Mansfield* in *Observer*.

18 'The Politics of Starvation' in *Tribune*.

19 'Songs We Used to Sing' in *Evening Standard*.

22 Tells Geoffrey Gorer he is dropping most journalism after May in order to concentrate on a novel [*Nineteen Eighty-Four*].

24 'The Intellectual Revolt' in *Manchester Evening News*.

31 'What is Socialism?' in *Manchester Evening News*.

February

7 (Thurs) 'The Christian Reformers' in *Manchester Evening News*.

8 'Books versus Cigarettes' in *Tribune*.

9 'The Moon under Water' in *Evening Standard*.

14 'Pacifism and Progress' in *Manchester Evening News*.

14   Publication of *Critical Essays*.

15   'Decline of the English Murder' in *Tribune*.

19   Repays £150 of the £300 loaned to him in 1938.

22   'Words and Henry Miller' in *Tribune*.

24   Reviews Tennyson Jesse's *The Story of Burma* in *Observer*.

March

Writes booklet on 'British Cookery' (unpublished).

4   (Mon) Writes to Tennyson Jesse summarising his Burmese experiences.

15   Reviews Winwood Reade's *The Martyrdom of Man* in *Tribune*.

16   Signs letter in *Forward* urging that the aim of the Nuremberg trials (of German war criminals) should be the establishment of historical truth.

22   'In Front of Your Nose' in *Tribune*.

29   Broadcast talk: 'The Voyage of the Beagle' (BBC Third Programme).

31   Tells Arthur Koestler he plans to go to Jura in May.

April

'Politics and the English Language' in *Horizon*.

1   (Mon) Addresses public meeting on 'Planning and Freedom' at Conway Hall, Holborn.

10 Visits Wallington for the first time since the death of his wife.

11 Reviews *The Ingoldsby Legends* in *Manchester Evening News*.

12 'Some Thoughts on the Common Toad' in *Tribune*.

13 Declines to serve as President of the British branch of PEN, the international writers' organisation.

25 Pickford's move his goods from Wallington to Jura.

26 'A Good Word for the Vicar of Bray' in *Tribune*.

29 Publication of US edition of *Critical Essays* (under the title *Dickens, Dali and Others*) by Reynal & Hitchcock, New York.

May

'Editorial' in *Polemic*.

'James Burnham and the Managerial Revolution' in *Polemic*.

3 (Fri) Death of his elder sister Marjorie, aged 48.

3 'Confessions of a Book Reviewer' in *Tribune*.

4 Sends copy of Trotsky's *Life of Stalin* to Fredric Warburg. To Nottingham for Marjorie's funeral.

23 Arrives at Barnhill, a house he has rented on the island of Jura. Stays here until 13 October.

31 His sister Avril arrives to act as housekeeper.

June

'Why I Write' in *Gangrel*.

July

Early in the month returns to London to bring Richard to Jura.

August

Begins writing *Nineteen Eighty-Four* (under the title 'The Last Man in Europe').

26 (Mon) Publication of US edition of *Animal Farm* by Harcourt Brace, New York.

September

'The Cost of Letters' in *Horizon*.

'Politics versus Literature: An Examination of *Gulliver's Travels*' in *Polemic*.

28 (Sat) Tells George Woodcock he is 'ashamed' of *Keep the Aspidistra Flying* and *A Clergyman's Daughter*.

October

13 (Sun) Returns to London.

November

Ceases book reviewing for *Manchester Evening News*.

Recommences 'As I Please' column in *Tribune*.

'How the Poor Die' in *Now*.

2 (Sat) Writes to Leonard Moore accepting *New Yorker's* proposals for reprinting his articles and reviews.

22 'Riding Down from Bangor' in *Tribune*.

December

29 (Sun) To Jura.

1947

January

8 (Wed) Returns to London.

14 *Animal Farm* adapted for radio by George Orwell (BBC Third Programme).

31 'As I Pleased' in *Tribune*, a summary of his relations with the paper.

March

'Lear, Tolstoy and the Fool' in *Polemic*.

14 (Fri) Asks Victor Gollancz if he can be released from his contract with Gollancz (Orwell had contracted to let Gollancz have first refusal of his novels).

25 Writes again to Victor Gollancz requesting termination of his contract.

29 'Burnham's View of the Contemporary World Struggle' in New York *New Leader*.

April

Early in April, Victor Gollancz agrees to cancellation of Orwell's contract.

4 (Fri) Final appearance of his 'As I Please' column (his 80th column).

9 Thanks Victor Gollancz for his 'generous action'.

11 Arrives on Jura with Avril Blair and Richard (until 20 December).

12 Writes to Sonia Brownell inviting her to visit Jura.

May

31 (Sat) Sends 'Such, Such Were the Joys' to Fredric Warburg.

31 Tells Fredric Warburg he has written one-third of the rough draft of *Nineteen Eighty-Four*.

June

Reads Hesketh Pearson's biography of Oscar Wilde.

July

'Toward European Unity' in *Partisan Review*.

Richard Rees arrives on Jura early in July and stays until the end of September.

August

17 (Sun)–19 Goes on a boat trip to Glengarrisdale Bay on the other side of the island; on the return journey is nearly drowned in the whirlpool of Corryvreckan.

September

Orwell gives up the Wallington cottage, intending to make Jura his summer home and keep his Islington flat as his London base.

Increasingly ill with lung problems during September and October.

October

Prepares *Coming Up for Air* as the first volume in a uniform edition of his works to be published by Secker & Warburg.

22 (Wed) Returns corrected proofs of *Coming Up for Air*.

23 Tells Anthony Powell he is unable to review Gissing's *A Life's Morning* due to pressure of work.

31 Has to work in bed due to illness.

November

7 (Fri) Completes first draft of *Nineteen Eighty-Four*.

December

Orwell is advised to enter a sanatorium for at least four months.

'The Three Best Books of 1947' in *Horizon* [George Orwell nominates Conrad's *Under Western Eyes*, James's *The Aspern Papers* and Trollope's *Framley Parsonage* as the best books he has read during the year].

20   (Sat) Leaves Jura en route for Glasgow.

24   Admitted to Hairmyres Hospital, East Kilbride, Glasgow, suffering from tuberculosis. Stays until 28 July 1948.

1948

January

2   (Fri) Tells Julian Symons he has agreed to write book reviews for the *Observer* once a fortnight.

February

1   (Sun) Asks David Astor for his help in obtaining streptomycin to speed recovery of tuberculosis.

4   Tells Fredric Warburg he hopes to finish writing *Nineteen Eighty-Four* by the end of the year.

15   'Marx and Russia' in *Observer*.

March

Writes 'Writers and Leviathan'.

5   (Fri) Thanks John Middleton Murry for sending *The Free Society*.

21   Tells Julian Symons his recent reading has included

the minor novels of Charlotte Brontë, and Mauriac's *Thérèse Desqueyroux*.

23 Thanks George Woodcock for sending his volume of poetry, *Imagine the South*.

April

Corrects proofs for a reprint of *Burmese Days*.

20 (Tues) Tells Julian Symons he is planning a long article on George Gissing and thinks *The Odd Women* is one of the best novels in English.

24 Writes to George Woodcock commenting on his poetry.

May

Begins second draft of *Nineteen Eighty-Four*.

Writes essay 'George Gissing'.

9 (Sun) Reviews Oscar Wilde's *The Soul of Man under Socialism* in *Observer*.

10 Tells Julian Symons (apropos *Coming Up for Air*) 'I am not a real novelist anyway'.

13 Publication of *Coming Up for Air*, the first volume in a uniform edition.

24 Thanks George Woodcock for his book of essays, *The Writer and Politics*.

27 Tells Celia Kirwan his health has greatly improved, though he is 'frightfully weak and thin'.

June

25 (Fri) Orwell's 45th birthday. Tells Anthony Powell 'I seem to be getting quite back into the journalistic mill.'

July

Reviews Osbert Sitwell's *Great Morning* in *Adelphi*.

10 (Sat) Tells Julian Symons his recent reading has included Graham Greene's *The Heart of the Matter*, Evelyn Waugh's *The Loved One* and Farrell's *Studs Lonigan*.

17 Reviews Graham Greene's *The Heart of the Matter* in *New Yorker*.

28 Returns to Jura, where he continues work on *Nineteen Eighty-Four*. Remains until January 1949.

August

1 (Sun) 'For Ever Eton' in *Observer* (a review of B. J. W. Hill's *Eton Medley*).

September

18 (Sat) Signs letter in *Socialist Leader* appealing for support for the Freedom Defence Committee.

October

'Britain's Struggle for Survival' in *Commentary*.

'The Labour Government After Three Years' in *Commentary*.

22 (Fri) Tells Fredric Warburg he is hesitating between *Nineteen Eighty-Four* and *The Last Man in Europe* as the title of his novel, which he hopes to finish in November.

29 Tells Julian Symons he has been ill again for the past month.

November

Finishes writing *Nineteen Eighty-Four*, then types it himself. Throughout November and December is confined indoors.

7 (Sun) Reviews Jean-Paul Sartre's *Portrait of the Antisemite* in *Observer*.

15 Publication of *British Pamphleteers*, with Introduction by George Orwell.

15 Tells Anthony Powell he is planning to spend winter in a sanatorium.

19 Tells Leonard Moore he has decided to type *Nineteen Eighty-Four* himself.

28 Reviews T. S. Eliot's *Notes towards the Definition of Culture* in *Observer*.

December

4 (Sat) Finishes typing fair copy of *Nineteen Eighty-Four* and posts completed manuscript.

18 Tells Tosco Fyvel 'Everything is going well here except me.'

21 Tells Fredric Warburg he should have entered a sanatorium earlier but was anxious to complete work on *Nineteen Eighty-Four*.

24　Final entry in domestic diary.

1949

January

'Reflections on Gandhi' in *Partisan Review*.

During this year Orwell makes notes for a novella, 'A Smoking Room Story', and also for essays on Conrad and Waugh. Becomes member of PEN.

2　(Sun) Leaves Jura en route for sanatorium.

6　Admitted to Cotswold Sanatorium, Cranham, Gloucestershire (until 3 September).

17　Tells Reginald Reynolds he has been reading the Hammonds' *The English Labourer*.

21　Fredric Warburg visits Orwell. *Nineteen Eighty-Four* is finalised as the title of the novel.

28　Asks Richard Rees for his help in correcting proofs of *Nineteen Eighty-Four*.

February

Begins writing essay on 'Evelyn Waugh' for *Partisan Review* (not completed).

Reads Bertrand Russell's *Human Knowledge: Its Scope and Limits* and Cecil Delisle Burns's *The First Europe*.

2　(Wed) Tells Julian Symons he is trying to persuade Warburg to reprint some Gissing titles, for which he would write introductions.

4 Asks Julian Symons to send a copy of his thriller *Bland Beginning*.

6 Reviews F. R. Leavis's *The Great Tradition* in *Observer*.

9 Jacintha Buddicom writes to him after losing contact since 1922.

14 Writes friendly letter to Jacintha Buddicom.

March

Corrects proofs of *Nineteen Eighty-Four*.

Reads Evelyn Waugh's *Rossetti* and *Robbery under Law*, Hesketh Pearson's *Dickens*, Israel Zangwill's *Children of the Ghetto* and Thomas Hardy's *Tess of the D'Urbervilles* and *Jude the Obscure*.

3 (Thurs) Publishes letter in *News Chronicle* appealing on behalf of Enrique Nadal, a Spanish Republican under sentence of death.

15 Sends Hesketh Pearson's *Dickens* to Julian Symons.

17 Tells Leonard Moore he cannot agree to *Nineteen Eighty-Four* being abbreviated or altered for the American edition.

30 Tells Fredric Warburg he considers Zamyatin's *We* to be better written than London's *The Iron Heel*.

31 Tells Richard Rees he intends to make a will and also to leave notes for his literary executors.

April

Reads Ruth Fischer's *Stalin and German Communism*, Margarete Neumann's *Under Two Dictators*, Richard Cargoe's *The Tormentors*, R. S. Surtees's *Mr Sponge's Sporting Tour* and Dickens's *Little Dorrit*.

Writes essay on Evelyn Waugh (left unfinished).

8   (Fri) Receives cable advising him that *Nineteen Eighty-Four* will be US Book of the Month Club choice.

9   Ceases book reviewing for *Observer*.

10   'Conrad's Place and Rank in English Letters' in the Polish literary journal *Wiadomosci*.

May

Reads Anthony Powell's *Brief Lives: and Other Selected Writings of John Aubrey* and Hugh Kingsmill's *The Sentimental Journey: A Life of Charles Dickens*.

'The Question of the Pound Award' in *Partisan Review*.

11   (Wed) Tells Anthony Powell he considers Hugh Kingsmill's biography of Dickens 'a brilliant book'.

14   Reviews Winston Churchill's *Their Finest Hour* in *New Leader* (New York).

15   'Mr Dickens Sits for his Portrait' in *New York Times Book Review*, (a review of Hesketh Pearson's *Dickens*).

15   Death of Hugh Kingsmill.

18   Jacintha Buddicom writes again to ask if he needs books or jigsaw puzzles.

22 Tells Jacintha Buddicom 'I've been most horribly ill and am not very grand now.'

June

6 (Mon) Tells Anthony Powell he is sorry to hear of Kingsmill's death and is keen to be of practical help. He is reading Dante 'with a crib of course'.

8 Publication of *Nineteen Eighty-Four* in an edition of 25,500 copies.

13 Publication of US edition of *Nineteen Eighty-Four* by Harcourt Brace, New York.

15 Fredric Warburg visits him and discusses possible future projects.

16 Tells a correspondent that *Nineteen Eighty-Four* is a satire and that *'totalitarianism, if not fought against,* could triumph anywhere'.

16 Thanks Julian Symons for his favourable review of *Nineteen Eighty-Four* (*Times Literary Supplement*, 10 June 1949).

July

Nineteen Eighty-Four is chosen by the American Book of the Month Club.

Sonia Brownell agrees to marry him.

28 (Thurs) Tells Richard Rees that *Animal Farm* has been translated into Russian.

August

Begins planning a volume of reprinted essays [*Shooting an Elephant*].

22 (Mon) Tells Fredric Warburg he has sketched out his book of essays but wishes to include new essays on Conrad and Gissing, not yet written.

September

3 (Sat) Transfers to University College Hospital, Gower Street, London WC1.

17 Tells Philip Rahv 'I have hardly set pen to paper since last December.'

27 Malcolm Muggeridge visits him; Orwell discusses H. G. Wells.

October

Condensed version of *Nineteen Eighty-Four* is published by Readers' Digest.

6 (Thurs) Muggeridge visits him and discusses politics.

11 Tells Leonard Moore 'I am still very weak and ill, but I think better on the whole.'

13 Marries Sonia Brownell in a ceremony held at the hospital. David Astor is best man.

December

During 1949 Orwell has read 144 books, of which he has read 27 before.

1950

January

Plans to leave England and travel to a Swiss sanatorium. He is due to travel on 25 January.

18 (Wed) Makes his will. His wife Sonia and Richard Rees are named as his literary executors.

21 Dies of pulmonary tuberculosis, aged 46.

26 Funeral service at Christ Church, Albany Street, London NW1, followed by burial at the parish church of All Saints, Sutton Courtenay, Oxfordshire.

The Orwell Circle

Anand, Mulk Raj (1905–), Indian novelist and critic. Anand broadcast for the Indian section of the BBC during the Second World War, when he and George Orwell worked closely together. His most well known novel is *Untouchable* (1935).

Astor, David (1912–1993), editor. Astor was foreign editor of the *Observer* from 1946–48, when he became editor. He and Orwell met early in the Second World War and became friends. Astor was the best man at Orwell's marriage to Sonia Brownell and was instrumental in arranging for Orwell to be buried at Sutton Courtenay, Oxfordshire, where the Astor family had an estate.

Blair, Avril Nora (1908–78), younger sister of George Orwell. For many years she kept a teashop at Southwold, Suffolk. After the death of Orwell's wife Eileen, Avril became his housekeeper and helped to look after his adopted son Richard. In 1951 she married William (Bill) Dunn, who had farmed land at Barnhill on the island of Jura, and moved with him to the mainland of Scotland. She recorded her memories of her brother in 'My Brother, George Orwell' (*Twentieth Century*, March 1961).

Blair, Ida Mabel, née Limouzin (1875–1943), mother of George Orwell. Widely read, vivacious and imaginative, she was the daughter of a French father and an English mother. Born in Burma, she married Richard Blair in 1896 and settled in England from 1904 onwards, living first at Henley-on-Thames and later (1921 onwards) at Southwold on the Suffolk coast. Unconventional and adaptable, she was in many ways the temperamental opposite of her more stolid husband.

Blair, Marjorie Frances (1898–1946), older sister of George Orwell. In 1920 she married Humphrey Dakin, a childhood friend, and settled with him at Headingley, Leeds. Orwell stayed with them while writing the draft of *Down and Out in Paris and London* and also while researching *The Road to Wigan Pier*.

Blair, Richard Horatio (1944–), adopted son of George Orwell. Orwell and his wife Eileen adopted Richard in June 1944 when he was aged three weeks. Following Eileen's death in March 1945 Richard was brought up by Orwell's sister Avril, first on the island of Jura then, after her marriage in 1951, on the mainland of Scotland. He is now an agricultural engineer.

Blair, Richard Walmesley (1857–1939), father of George Orwell. An official in the Opium Department of the Government of India, he served in that Department from the age of eighteen (1875) until his retirement in 1912 when he settled in England. During the First World War he was commissioned as a second lieutenant in the Army and posted to Marseilles. A sincere and well-meaning man, he displayed little interest in Orwell's literary activities.

Brownell, Sonia (1918–80), second wife of George Orwell. An editorial secretary of *Horizon* from 1945–50, she first met Orwell in 1945. She married Orwell in October 1949 and became one of his literary executors after his death in January 1950. With the assistance of Richard Rees and David Astor she established the Orwell Archive at University College Library, London, opened in 1960, and did much to further Orwell's literary reputation. Together with Ian Angus she edited *The Collected Essays, Journalism and Letters of George Orwell* in four volumes (1968).

Buddicom, Jacintha May (1901–93), childhood friend of George Orwell. She and her brother Prosper and sister

Guinever first met Orwell in the summer of 1914 at the village of Shiplake, near Henley, Oxfordshire. The Buddicom children befriended Orwell and from then until 1921 regularly spent school holidays together. After Orwell left for Burma in 1922, Jacintha lost touch with him, but they resumed correspondence in 1949. She recorded her impressions of him in *Eric and Us: A Remembrance of George Orwell*, published in 1974.

Collings, Dennis (1905–), civil servant. A friend of Orwell's from 1927 onwards, his father was the Blairs' family doctor at Southwold. He married Eleanor Jaques, another friend of Orwell, in 1934.

Common, Jack (1903–68) writer. Common became assistant editor of *Adelphi* in 1932 and editor from 1935–36. He wrote a number of autobiographical works including *The Freedom of the Streets* and *The Ampersand*. He met Orwell when the latter was a young reviewer for *Adelphi* and the two remained friends. Common lived in the Orwells' cottage at Wallington while Orwell was in Marrakesh (September 1938–April 1939).

Connolly, Cyril (1903–74), author and critic. Connolly was a contemporary of Orwell's at St Cyprian's school, Eastbourne, and at Eton. The editor of the influential literary journal *Horizon* from 1939–50, Connolly was a perceptive critic who gave Orwell encouragement and practical help. He was the author of a novel, *The Rock Pool* (1936), and several volumes of essays, including *Enemies of Promise* (1938), *The Condemned Playground* (1945) and *The Evening Colonnade* (1973). He remained a friend of Orwell's until the latter's death in 1950.

Cottman, Stafford (1918–). The youngest member of the Independent Labour Party contingent which fought alongside the POUM militia in which Orwell served during the Spanish

Civil War, Cottman was with Orwell when he escaped from Barcelona in May 1937. He met Orwell again later that year at the ILP Summer School at Letchworth.

Dunn, William (Bill), (1921–92), farmer. A former army officer, Dunn settled on the island of Jura in 1947 and joined Orwell and his sister Avril at Barnhill, where Dunn farmed the land. After Orwell's death he married Avril and together they brought up George Orwell's adopted son Richard.

Eliot, Thomas Stearns (1888–1965), poet and critic. George Orwell and Eliot first corresponded in 1931 when Eliot was a director of the publishing house Faber & Faber. He rejected *Down and Out* on the grounds that it was too short and fragmentary, and later rejected *Animal Farm*. Despite this, the two became friends during the war and frequently corresponded on literary matters connected with Orwell's broadcasts. Orwell strongly admired Eliot's poetry; in an autobiographical note written in 1940 he described Eliot as one of the modern writers 'I care most about and never grow tired of'.

Empson, William (1906–84), poet and critic. The author of a seminal work of literary criticism, *Seven Types of Ambiguity* (1930), he and Orwell worked closely together at the BBC during the years 1941–43. After the Second World War, Orwell often visited Empson and his wife Hetta at their home at Hampstead. Empson later became Professor of English Literature at Sheffield University.

Fierz, Mabel (1890–1990), reviewer. Born in Brazil, she settled in England in 1908 and met Orwell in Southwold in 1930. She and her husband Francis had many literary interests and she wrote book reviews for Richard Rees's journal *Adelphi*. Orwell was a frequent visitor to her home at 16 Oakwood Road, Hampstead Garden Suburb. She was of considerable practical help to him, most notably by rescuing the manuscript of *Down and Out in Paris and London* from destruction and persuading the literary agent Leonard Moore to accept it.

Fyvel, Tosco (1907–85), author, journalist and broadcaster. Fyvel was introduced to Orwell by Fredric Warburg in January 1940 and became a friend and correspondent. He succeeded Orwell as literary editor of *Tribune*, and wrote a critical study of Orwell under the title *George Orwell: A Personal Memoir* (1982). Fyvel was one of the group who lunched regularly with Orwell in the 1940s: the others were Julian Symons, Malcolm Muggeridge and Arthur Koestler.

Gollancz, Victor (1893–1967), publisher. A vigorous and idiosyncratic man, Gollancz founded the publishing house named after himself in 1927. He published George Orwell's first book *Down and Out in Paris and London*, in January 1933, and thereafter accepted all Orwell's titles until *Homage to Catalonia*, which he rejected on political grounds. Throughout the 1930's Gollancz developed a specialisation in socialist and pacifist books, founding the Left Book Club in 1936. He commissioned Orwell to write a report on the condition of the unemployed in the North of England, a book which became *The Road to Wigan Pier*. Following his rejection of *Animal Farm* in 1945, Orwell transferred his allegiance to Secker and Warburg. Gollancz was knighted in 1965.

Gorer, Geoffrey (1905–85), anthropologist. Gorer's friendship with George Orwell began when he wrote to Orwell praising *Burmese Days*. He wrote a favourable review of *Homage to Catalonia*, was instrumental in recommending Orwell to the influential *Time and Tide*, and remained friends until Orwell's death. Gorer is mainly remembered today for his important study *Exploring English Character*.

Gow, Andrew S. F. (1886–1978), scholar. George Orwell's tutor at Eton, he later became a Fellow of Trinity College,

Cambridge, Orwell's nickname for him was 'Wog'. Gow was an occasional correspondent in later years.

Heppenstall, Rayner (1911–81), novelist, poet and critic. He and George Orwell met in 1935 through their mutual friend Richard Rees. Later that year they shared a flat with the writer Michael Sayers at 50 Lawford Road, Kentish Town (August 1935–January 1936). Heppenstall recorded his memoirs of George Orwell in *Four Absentees* (1960).

Holden, Inez (1904–74), novelist and journalist. A cousin of Celia Kirwan (q.v.), Holden was introduced to George Orwell in 1940 by Fredric Warburg. She and Orwell became friends and correspondents. When his flat, 10a Mortimer Crescent, was bombed in 1944, Inez Holden lent her flat at 106 George Street for temporary use by the Orwells. Originally Orwell planned to publish his 'War Time Diary' in collaboration with Holden, but her diary was published separately under the title *It Was Different At The Time* (1945).

Hollis, Christopher (1902–77), author. Hollis knew George Orwell at Eton, although, unlike Runciman and King-Farlow, he was not in the same Election. He wrote a perceptive study of Orwell, *A Study of George Orwell* (1956), which contains an excellent chapter on life in College at Eton. Hollis became a writer and a Member of Parliament.

Jackson, Lydia (1899–1983), writer. Born in Russia, she came to England in 1925. She met Eileen O'Shaughnessy in 1934 at University College, London, and befriended both Eileen and Orwell. She wrote under the pseudoym 'Elisaveta Fen'. After the Orwells left Wallington in 1940, the house there was let to her, and she continued to live there until 1947.

Jaques, Eleanor (1906–62). The Jaques family originated in Canada and settled at Southwold in 1921, where they were neighbours of the Blairs. Eleanor became a friend and correspondent of George Orwell and during 1932–33 had a love affair with him. She married Dennis Collings in 1934. Aspects of her personality are reflected in the character 'Rosemary' in *Keep the Aspidistra Flying*.

King-Farlow, Denys (1903–82), oil trader. An exact contemporary of George Orwell at Eton, he worked with Orwell on two literary magazines, *Election Times* and *College Days*. After friendship at Eton, the two lost touch until 1936, when King-Farlow contacted Orwell again. The two resumed their friendship and met and corresponded at intervals until Orwell's death.

Kirwan, Celia, née Paget (1916–   ), editor. The twin sister of Arthur Koestler's wife Mamaine, she became editorial assistant of the journal *Polemic* in the 1940s. She and George Orwell became friends and correspondents.

Koestler, Arthur (1905–83), novelist and critic. Koestler read and admired *Homage to Catalonia* and George Orwell favourably reviewed his *Spanish Testament*. They became close friends and frequently corresponded on political and philosophical matters. Orwell was deeply impressed with Koestler's *Darkness at Noon* (1940), a novel which anticipates some of the themes of *Nineteen Eighty-Four*.

Kopp, Georges (1902–51), engineer and soldier. Kopp was George Orwell's battalion commander on the Aragon front during the Spanish Civil War and befriended both Orwell and his wife Eileen. When Kopp was imprisoned by Communist forces in Barcelona, Orwell tried to secure his release. Kopp later joined the French Foreign Legion and eventually settled in Britain, marrying Eileen's half-sister.

Limouzin, Nellie (c. 1880–1950), aunt of George Orwell. The sister of Orwell's mother Ida, she left England in the 1920s and moved to Paris, where she lived with her husband Eugene Adam, a socialist and Esperantist. Orwell visited her during his sojourn in Paris and later they corresponded on literary topics. Bohemian and intellectual, her company was greatly enjoyed by Orwell.

McNair, John (1887–1968), political secretary. The General Secretary of the Independent Labour Party from 1939–55, he was the ILP representative in Barcelona during the Spanish Civil War. He and George Orwell escaped from Spain together. Later he wrote a biography of James Maxton, *The Beloved Rebel*. He was for many years a regular contributor to the ILP journal *The Socialist Leader*.

Miller, Henry (1891–1980), novelist and essayist. The author of numerous novels including *Tropic of Cancer* (1934) and *Tropic of Capricorn* (1939), he and George Orwell met in Paris on the eve of Orwell's involvement in the Spanish Civil War. Orwell admired Miller's direct and uninhibited style; he discusses his work in *Inside the Whale*.

Moore, Leonard (?–1959), literary agent. The principal figure in the firm of Christy and Moore, he began to correspond with George Orwell in April 1932 when Mabel Fierz persuaded him to accept the manuscript of *Down and Out in Paris and London*. From then until Orwell's death, Moore continued to act as Orwell's literary agent, negotiating with publishers on Orwell's behalf and advising him on contractual matters.

Muggeridge, Malcolm (1903–90), journalist. A correspondent for the *Manchester Guardian* from 1930–3, he later joined the editorial staff of the *Evening Standard* and became editor of *Punch*. He and Anthony Powell lunched regularly with George Orwell during the years following the Second World War, and visited Orwell during the latter's final illnesses.

Murry, John Middleton (1889–1957), editor and critic. Following the death of his wife Katherine Mansfield, Murry founded the magazine *Adelphi* in 1923 and owned it until 1948. Murry was a convinced pacifist and his views rarely coincided with Orwell's. Despite disagreeing on this and other issues, the two corresponded on political and literary topics.

Myers, Leo Hamilton (1881–1944), novelist. The son of the poet F. W. H. Myers, he possessed a private income which enabled him to devote his whole time to writing. Mainly remembered today for his novel *The Near and the Far* (1929) and its sequels, he and George Orwell first met in 1938, when Orwell had been advised to seek a warmer climate. Myers arranged to advance £300 to Max and Dorothy Plowman, asking them to pass it on to Orwell as an anonymous gift. Orwell insisted on regarding it as a loan, and he and Myers later became friends.

O'Shaughnessy, Eileen Maud (1905–45), first wife of George Orwell. Born in South Shields and educated at Sunderland High School, she read English at St Hugh's College, Oxford, and became a teacher and journalist. She and Orwell met in 1935, when she was studying psychology at University College, London. She married Orwell in 1936 and moved with him to Wallington, Hertfordshire. During the Spanish Civil War she served for a brief period in the Independent Labour Party office in Barcelona, and in the Second World War she worked in the Censorship Department in Whitehall. She assisted him in all his activities and was a devoted wife and companion. She died in 1945, aged 39, while awaiting a hysterectomy operation.

O'Shaughnessy, Gwen, doctor. Sister-in-law of George Orwell's wife Eileen, she arranged for the Orwells to adopt the baby boy they named Richard Horatio Blair. She provided George Orwell with friendship and support, particularly after his wife's death.

O'Shaughnessy, Laurence Eric, surgeon. The brother of George Orwell's wife Eileen, he was a distinguished Professor at the Royal College of Surgeons, a chest and heart specialist who provided Orwell with valuable advice on tubercular problems. He went to France with the British Expeditionary Force in 1940 and was killed during the Dunkirk evacuation.

Peters, Richard Stanley (1919–), writer and educationalist. The son of C. R. Peters, an officer in the Indian Imperial Police, he later became Professor of the Philosophy of Education at the University of London. He was one of three boys tutored by George Orwell at Southwold in 1930 and 1931, and wrote his impressions of Orwell in 'A Boy's View of George Orwell' in *Psychology and Ethical Development* (1974). Peters has been a dominant figure in the development of philosophical studies of education and has written monographs on Rousseau and Hobbes.

Pitter, Ruth (1897–1992), poet. A friend of the Blair family, especially of George Orwell's older sister Marjorie, she was instrumental in finding him lodgings on Portobello Road, London, when he returned to England in 1928. She was the author of several volumes of poetry including *Persephone in Hades* (1932) and *The Spirit Watches* (1940), both of which he reviewed in *Adelphi*. She described his early attempts to write fiction as 'like a cow with a musket'.

Plowman, Max (1883–1941) writer. A member of the editorial staff of *Adelphi* from 1929–41, Plowman gave George Orwell much encouragement in his early writing. He and his wife Dorothy were lifelong friends of Orwell.

Potts, Paul (1911–), poet. Canadian by birth, Potts met George Orwell in 1944 and became a firm friend and admirer. He visited Orwell on Jura and wrote his reminiscences of Orwell in *Dante Called You Beatrice* (1960).

Powell, Anthony (1905–), novelist. A contemporary of George Orwell at Eton, the two men met again in 1941 and remained friends until Orwell's death. Powell admired George Orwell's novel *Keep the Aspidistra Flying* and became a frequent correspondent. He is principally remembered today for his twelve-volume novel sequence *A Dance to the Music of Time* (1951–75).

Pritchett, Victor Sawdon (1900–), novelist, critic and short story writer. Pritchett and George Orwell met in 1940 and became friends. He wrote a highly favourable review of *The Lion and the Unicorn* and also broadcast a profile of Orwell on the BBC Third Programme (included in *Living Writers*, edited by Gilbert Phelps, 1949). He wrote a fine obituary in the *New Statesman* (28 January 1950), describing Orwell as 'the wintry conscience of a generation'. Pritchett wrote two volumes of autobiography, *The Cab at the Door* and *Midnight Oil*.

Rahv, Philip (1908–73), editor and critic. Rahv founded the American literary journal *Partisan Review* in 1934 and became its co-editor. He and George Orwell frequently corresponded on literary and topical issues.

Read, Sir Herbert (1893–1968), poet and critic. The author of several volumes of literary criticism and verse, Read and George Orwell worked closely together during Orwell's tenure at the BBC (1941–43). Read was Chairman of the Freedom Defence Committee, founded in 1945 to protect the civil liberties of British subjects.

Rees, Sir Richard (1900–70), author, critic and painter. He edited *Adelphi* from 1930–36 and gave George Orwell practical help and encouragement, particularly during the crucial early phase of Orwell's literary career. Orwell was a frequent visitor to Rees's flat at 33 Cheyne Walk, London SW3, often using it as a base to change into tramping clothes for his 'down and out' expeditions. The character 'Ravelston' in *Keep the Aspidistra Flying* is in part a fictional portrait of Rees. Rees was a steadfast friend, frequently meeting Orwell in London and on the island of Jura. He wrote a perceptive study of Orwell, *George Orwell: Fugitive from the Camp of Victory* (1961).

Richards, Vernon (1915–), editor and journalist. The editor of *Spain and the World* (and its successor *Revolt*), Richards was editor of the anarchist journal *Freedom* from 1939–49. He was a friend and correspondent of George Orwell in the 1940s.

Runciman, Steven (1903–), historian. An exact contemporary of George Orwell in College at Eton, he later became a noted authority on Byzantine civilisation. His works include *A History of the Crusades*, The *Sicilian Vespers* and *The Fall of Constantinople*. He was knighted in 1958.

Salkeld, Brenda (1903–), teacher. She met George Orwell at Southwold in 1928 and remained friends with him until his death. The two frequently corresponded on literary topics; the friendship was particularly important to him during the years 1932–34 when he was seeking to establish himself as a writer. She visited him at Jura and during his final illnesses.

Senhouse, Roger (1900–65), publisher. Senhouse was a director of the publishing house Secker & Warburg. He and George Orwell corresponded frequently from 1947 onwards on matters connected with *Nineteen Eighty-Four* and with the publication of a uniform edition of Orwell's works.

Spender, Stephen (1909–95), poet and critic. Spender met George Orwell in 1938 and the two became good friends. At first Orwell had misunderstood Spender, describing him as a 'parlour Bolshevik', but after meeting him Orwell apologised for the misrepresentation. Spender visited Orwell regularly during the latter's final illness and recorded his memoirs of Orwell in *The Thirties and After* (1978).

Struve, Gleb (1898–1985), scholar. A Russian by birth, Struve was a specialist in Soviet literature and taught at the School of Slavonic Studies in London from 1932–47. He was the author of *Twenty-Five Years of Soviet Russian Literature* and *Russian Literature in Exile*. He and George Orwell began corresponding in 1944, and it was Struve who introduced Orwell to Zamyatin's novel *We* (a seminal influence on *Nineteen Eighty-Four*) which Orwell first read in the same year.

Symons, Julian (1912–94), novelist, biographer and critic. He founded and edited *Twentieth Century Verse* (1937–39), an important poetry magazine, and wrote numerous volumes of biography, including studies of Dickens, Carlyle, Poe and Conan Doyle. Now mainly remembered as a crime novelist, he met George Orwell during the Second World War and the two became friends and correspondents. He wrote a perceptive review of *Nineteen Eighty-Four* (*Times Literary Supplement*, 10 June 1949) which pleased Orwell greatly.

Warburg, Fredric (1898–1980), publisher. The managing director of the publishing house Secker & Warburg, he became George Orwell's publisher after Gollancz declined to accept *Homage to Catalonia*. He earned Orwell's lasting friendship when he agreed to publish *Animal Farm* after several other firms had rejected it. Warburg recorded his memories of Orwell in two autobiographical volumes, *An Occupation for Gentlemen* and *All Authors are Equal*.

Watson, Susan (1918–), housekeeper. Susan Watson, née Henderson, became George Orwell's housekeeper in 1945 and looked after his adopted son Richard after Eileen's death. She was employed first at Canonbury Square, Islington, and later at Jura. Her reminiscences of Orwell are contained in the volume *Orwell Remembered*, edited by Audrey Coppard and Bernard Crick (1984).

Wells, Herbert George (1866–1946), writer. As a young man, George Orwell greatly admired Wells's fiction, particularly *A Modern Utopia* and *The Country of the Blind and Other Stories*. In 1941 Orwell wrote an important critical essay, 'Wells, Hitler and the World State', which acknowledged Wells's literary significance but argued that he underestimated the role of prejudice and irrationality. The two met on several occasions during the Second World War, and Orwell adapted the short story 'A Slip Under the Microscope' for radio (6 October 1943).

Wilkes, Cicely Ellen Vaughan (1875–1967), teacher. The headmaster's wife and joint proprietor of St Cyprian's school, Eastbourne, from 1900–39, Mrs Wilkes exercised the real power at the school and was involved in every aspect of school life. In his memoir of St Cyprian's, 'Such, Such were the Joys', George Orwell portrayed her as tyrannical, but other contemporaries remembered her as kindly and motherly. Cyril Connolly recorded his memories of the school in *Enemies of Promise*. St Cyprian's was destroyed by fire in 1939.

Woodcock, George (1912–95), poet and editor. He edited *Now* from 1940–47 and became editor of *Canadian Literature* in 1959. Though he and George Orwell disagreed in their attitude to pacifism ('Pacifism and the War', *Partisan Review*, September–October 1942), they became friends and correspondents. A former Professor of English at the University of British Columbia, he was the author of an important study of Orwell, *The Crystal Spirit* (1967).

Chronology of Orwell's Works

Down and Out in Paris and London. London, Gollancz, 1933; New York, Harper, 1933.

Burmese Days. New York, Harper, 1934; London, Gollancz, 1935.

A Clergyman's Daughter. London, Gollancz, 1935; New York, Harper, 1936.

Keep the Aspidistra Flying. London, Gollancz, 1936; New York, Harcourt Brace, 1956.

The Road to Wigan Pier. London, Gollancz, 1937; New York, Harcourt Brace, 1958.

Homage to Catalonia. London, Secker & Warburg, 1938; New York, Harcourt Brace, 1952.

Coming up for Air. London, Gollancz, 1939; New York, Harcourt Brace, 1950.

Inside the Whale. London, Gollancz, 1940.

The Lion and the Unicorn. London, Secker & Warburg, 1941.

Animal Farm. London, Secker & Warburg, 1945; New York, Harcourt Brace, 1946.

Critical Essays. London, Secker & Warburg, 1946. New York, Reynal & Hitchcock, 1946. (US title, *Dickens, Dali and Others*)

The English People. London, Collins, 1947.

Nineteen Eighty-Four. London, Secker & Warburg, 1949; New York, Harcourt Brace, 1949.

POSTHUMOUSLY PUBLISHED

Shooting an Elephant. London, Secker & Warburg, 1950; New York, Harcourt Brace, 1950.

Such, Such were the Joys. New York, Harcourt Brace, 1953.

England Your England. London, Secker & Warburg, 1953.

Collected Essays. London, Secker & Warburg, 1961.

The Collected Essays, Journalism and Letters. London, Secker & Warburg, 1968; New York, Harcourt Brace, 1968.

Orwell's London: A Chronology

Orwell lived at various addresses in or near London for much of his working life. The following chronology may be helpful:

Autumn 1927 – Spring 1928: 22 Portobello Road, Notting Hill.

October – November 1931: 2 Windsor Street, Paddington.

April 1932 – August 1933: The Hawthorns School for Boys, 116 Church Road, Hayes, Middlesex.

September – December 1933: Frays College, 65 Harefield Road, Uxbridge.

October 1934 – February 1935: 3 Warwick Mansions, Pond Street, Hampstead.

March – July 1935: 77 Parliament Hill, Hampstead.

August 1935 – January 1936: 50 Lawford Road, Kentish Town.

May 1940 – March 1941: 18 Dorset Chambers, Chagford Street, Regent's Park.

April 1941 – Summer 1942: 111 Langford Court, Abbey Road, St John's Wood.

Summer 1942 – June 1944: 10a Mortimer Crescent, Maida Vale.

July – October 1944: 106 George Street, off Baker Street.

October 1944 – December 1948: 27b Canonbury Square, Islington.

September 1949 – January 1950: University College Hospital, Gower Street.

Nineteen Eighty-Four: A Chronology

In view of the widespread popular and critical interest in Orwell's dystopian novel *Nineteen Eighty-Four*, a chronology of its composition and publication may be helpful.

Composition

1. Mid 1940 to the end of 1943: initial conception and gathering of ideas.

2. End of 1943 or early 1944: preparation of outline (reproduced as an Appendix to Bernard Crick's biography).

3. Summer 1945: begins work on early draft.

4. Summer 1946: Orwell types fifty pages of manuscript.

5. Summer and Autumn 1947: writing and typing of first complete draft version.

6. Summer and Autumn 1948: revision and rewriting.

7. November–December 1948: preparation of final typewritten manuscript.

Publication

1. *Nineteen Eighty-Four* was published in June 1949 by Secker & Warburg, London, and in New York by Harcourt Brace.

2. The holograph manuscript (or all of it that survives) was published in facsimile by Secker & Warburg, London, and

M & S Press, Massachusetts, in 1984. The volume was edited by Peter Davison.

3. The definitive text of the novel was published by Secker & Warburg in 1987 and Penguin Books in 1989. This authoritative text was edited by Peter Davison.

Sources

My principal sources have been the two standard biographies of Orwell: *George Orwell: A Life* by Bernard Crick (1980) and *Orwell: The Authorised Biography* by Michael Shelden (1991).

Also indispensable have been: *The Collected Essays, Journalism and Letters of George Orwell*, edited by Sonia Orwell and Ian Angus (four volumes, 1968) and the two excellent studies by Peter Stansky and William Abrahams, *The Unknown Orwell* (1972) and *Orwell: The Transformation* (1979).

The following have also been consulted:

Buddicom, Jacintha: *Eric and Us: A Remembrance of George Orwell* (London, Leslie Frewin, 1974).

Coppard, Audrey and Crick, Bernard: *Orwell Remembered* (London, British Broadcasting Corporation, 1984).

Davison, Peter (ed.): *The Complete Works of George Orwell*, 20 volumes (London, Secker & Warburg, 1986–98).

Gross, Miriam (ed.): *The World of George Orwell* (London, Weidenfeld & Nicolson, 1971).

Hammond, J. R.: *A George Orwell Companion* (London, Macmillan, 1982).

Lewis, Peter: *George Orwell: The Road to 1984* (London, Heinemann, 1981).

Thompson, John: *Orwell's London* (New York, Shocken Books, 1985).

West, W. J. (ed.): *George Orwell: The War Broadcasts* (London, Penguin Books, 1987).

West, W. J. (ed.): *George Orwell: The War Commentaries* (London, Penguin Books, 1987).

Williams, Raymond: *Orwell* (London, William Collins, 1971).

Williams, Raymond (ed.): *George Orwell: A Collection of Critical Essays* (New Jersey, Prentice-Hall, 1974).

Woodcock, George: *The Crystal Spirit: A Study of George Orwell* (London, Cape, 1967).

Index

This index is divided into three sections:

1. The Works of George Orwell
2. People and Groups
3. Places

1. The Works of George Orwell
Books

Animal Farm, 66, 68, 69, 70, 74, 75, 82, 92, 107

Burmese Days, 16, 22, 23, 24, 25, 26, 27, 28, 29, 30, 31, 32, 33, 34, 86

Clergyman's Daughter, A 30, 32, 33, 39, 81

Critical Essays, 71, 72
Coming up for Air, 44, 47, 48, 49, 50, 51, 84, 86

Down and Out in Paris and London, xii, xvii, 16, 18, 19, 20, 21, 22, 23, 24, 25, 26, 27, 29, 34, 98, 102

English People, The, 66, 69

Homage to Catalonia, 43, 44, 45, 46, 49, 51, 99, 107

Inside the Whale, 52, 53

Keep the Aspidistra Flying, 33, 34, 35, 36, 38, 81, 101, 105, 106

Lion and the Unicorn, The, 56, 57

Nineteen Eighty Four, xii, xiv, 74, 75, 81, 83, 84, 85, 86, 87, 88, 89, 90, 92, 93, 106, 107, 113–14

Road to Wigan Pier, The, xi, xv, 35, 36, 37, 38, 39, 40, 41, 42, 99

Shooting an Elephant, 93

Essays and Poetry

Antisemitism in Britain, 73
Arthur Koestler, 71
Art of Donald McGill, The, 61
As I Please, 67, 81, 82, 83

As One Non-Combatant to Another, 65
Authors Deserve a New Deal, 75
Awake! Young Men of England, 4

Back to the Land, 71
Beggars of London, The, 17
Benefit of Clergy, 69
Bookshop Memories, 40
Books versus Cigarettes, 78
Boys' Weeklies, 53
Burnham's View of the Contemporary World Struggle, 82

Catastrophic Gradualism, 76
Charles Dickens, 51, 53
Charles Reade, 56
Clink, 23, 24
Common Lodging Houses, 25
Confessions of a Book Reviewer, 80
Conrad's Place and Rank in English Letters, 91
Cost of Letters, The, 81

Day in the Life of a Tramp, A, 17
Decline of the English Murder, 79
Democracy in the British Army, 52
Detective Story, The, 67
Dressed Man and a Naked Man, A, 29

Eye Witness in Barcelona, 43

Farthing Newspaper, A, 17
For Ever Eton, 87
Freedom of the Park, 77
Frontiers of Art and Propaganda, The, 59
Funny, but not Vulgar, 75

George Gissing, 86
Good Bad Books, 76
Good Word for the Vicar of Bray, A, 80

Hanging, A, 20, 21
Happy Vicar, A, 40
Hop-Picking, 22
How Long is a Short Story?, 71
How the Poor Die, 17, 81
Hundred Up, A, 68

In Defence of English Cooking, 77
In Defence of the Novel, 40
In Defence of P.G. Wodehouse, 74
In Front of your Nose, 79
Inside the Whale, 53

James Burnham and the Managerial Revolution, 80
John Galsworthy, 17

Kitchener, 5

Lear, Tolstoy and the Fool, 82
Lessons of War, The, 53
Limit to Pessimism, The, 54
Literature and the Left, 65
Literature and Totalitarianism, 59
London Letters, 57, 58, 59, 60, 61, 62, 68, 69, 70, 72, 74, 75
Looking Back on the Spanish War, 63

Man in Kid Gloves, The, 18
Mark Twain – The Licensed Jester, 67
Meaning of a Poem, The, 59
Mood of the Moment, 61
Moon Under Water, The, 78
My Country Right or Left, 56

Nice Cup of Tea, A, 78
No, Not One, 60

Nonsense Poetry, 77
Not Counting Niggers, 51
Notes on Nationalism, 76
Notes on the Way, 54

On a Ruined Farm, 31
On Kipling's Death, 35
Oysters and Brown Stout, 72

Pacifism and the War, 63
Pagan, The, 8
Pamphlet Literature, 64
Pleasure Spots, 78
Poet in Darkness, 72
Poetry and the Microphone, 72
Politics and the English
  Language, 79
Politics of Starvation, The, 78
Politics versus Literature, 81
Prevention of Literature, The, 78
Proletarian Writer, The, 57
Propaganda and Demotic
  Speech, 69
Prophecies of Fascism, 56

Question of the Pound Award,
  The, 91

Raffles and Miss Blandish, 71
Rediscovery of Europe, The, 61
Reflections on Ghandi, 89
Revenge is Sour, 76
Riding Down from Bangor, 82

Rudyard Kipling, 61
Ruling Class, The, 57

St Andrews Day 1935, 35
Shooting an Elephant, 38, 39
Some Thoughts on the Common
  Toad, 80
Sometimes in the Middle
  Autumn Days, 28
Spike, The, 18, 19, 20
Spilling the Spanish Beans, 43, 44
Sporting Spirit, The, 77
Such, Such were the Joys, xiv, 2,
  83, 108
Summer-Like, 28

Through a Glass Rosily, 77
Tobias Smollett, 71
Tolstoy and Shakespeare, 59
Toward European Unity, 83

W.B. Yeats, 64
War-Time Diary, 55, 100
Wells, Hitler and the World
  State, 59
What is Science?, 76
Who are the War Criminals?, 66
Why I Joined the Independent
  Labour Party, 47
Why I Write, 80
Why not War Writers?, 60
Writers and Leviathan, 85
You and the Atom Bomb, 76

2. People and Groups

Anand, Mulk Raj, 62
Astor, David, 85, 93

Bailey, L.I., 17, 18
Baudelaire, Charles, 29, 72
Blair, Avril Nora (sister), 2, 9, 11,
  80, 83

Blair, Eileen Maud, nee
  O'Shaughnessy (first wife),
  1, 33, 34, 38, 40, 41, 43,
  46, 47, 48, 49, 52, 54, 61,
  73
Blair, Ida Mabel (mother), 1, 2,
  11, 15, 30, 48, 65

Blair, Marjorie (sister), 1, 19, 23, 37, 80
Blair, Richard Horatio (adopted son), 69, 77, 81, 83, 103
Blair, Richard Walmesley (father), 1, 3, 7, 9, 11, 15, 51
Booklovers' Corner, 32, 35
British Broadcasting Corporation, 59, 60, 63, 64, 67
Brownell, Sonia (second wife), 77, 83, 92, 93, 94
Buddicom, Jacintha, 4, 7, 8, 9, 10, 11, 90, 91, 92
Buddicom, Prosper, 10
Burnham, James, 68, 80, 82
Butler, Samuel, 15, 74

Chesterton, G.K. 6
Churchill, Winston, 54, 59, 91
Collings, Dennis, 21, 22
Comfort, Alex, 65
Common, Jack, 37, 38, 46, 47, 48, 49, 62
Connolly, Cyril, 4, 5, 7, 34, 39, 42, 44, 46, 47, 49, 72
Conrad, Joseph, 39, 74, 85, 89, 91
Cripps, Sir Stafford, 62

Dakin, Humphrey, 19
Dickens, Charles, ix, 75, 90, 91
Doyle, Arthur Conan 6

Eliot, T.S., 22, 23, 63, 64, 88

Fierz, Mabel, 21, 23
Forster, E.M., 39

Galsworthy, John, 10, 17, 46
Gissing, George, 65, 84, 86, 90, 93

Gollancz, Victor, xii, 24, 31, 32, 33, 38, 40, 42, 43, 53, 68, 69, 82, 83
Gorer, Geoffrey, 43, 46, 50, 53, 54, 78
Greene, Graham, 69, 87

Hart, B.H. Liddell, 63, 64
Heppenstall, Rayner, 34, 70
Hess, Rudolf, 58
Hitler, Adolf, 27, 28, 48, 53, 56, 73
Hornung, E.W., 6

Jaques, Eleanor, 24, 25, 26, 27, 28, 29
James, Henry, 6, 85
James, M.R., 6, 11
Jellinek, Frank, 49, 50
Joyce, James, 28, 68

King-Farlow, Denys, 7
Kipling, Rudyard, 6, 11, 35, 61
Koestler, Arthur, 45, 70, 71, 77, 79

Lawrence, D.H., 11, 15, 29, 76
London, Jack, 11, 64, 76

Manchester Evening News, 67, 68, 69, 71, 73, 75, 76, 81
Miller, Henry, 35, 39, 40, 79
Moore, Leonard, 22, 23, 24, 25, 26, 27, 28, 29, 30, 31, 32, 33, 34, 35, 40, 43, 44, 49, 52, 53, 70, 72, 75, 82, 88, 90, 93
Mosley, Oswald, 37
Mumford, Lewis, 19
Murry, John Middleton, 70, 85
Myers, L.H., 47, 52

Observer, 67, 72, 73, 74, 85, 91

O'Hara, Kathleen, 15
O'Shaughnessy, Eileen, see Blair, Eileen
O'Shaughnessy, Laurence, 51, 55

Peters, C.R., 19
Pitter, Ruth, 15
Plowman, Max, 20, 59
Poe, Edgar Allan, xi, 11, 15
Potter, Beatrix, 2
Powell, Anthony, 38, 84, 87, 88, 91, 92
Priestley, J.B., 19

Reade, Charles, 56
Rees, Sir Richard, 38, 83, 89, 90, 92, 94
Runciman, Sir Steven, 7

Salkeld, Brenda, 25, 26, 28, 30, 31, 33
Sayers, Michael, 34
Shaw, George Bernard, 9, 28, 56, 64

Spender, Stephen, 44, 46, 59
Stevenson, R.L., 11, 77
Struve, Gleb, 68
Swift, Jonathan, 2, 6, 63, 81
 Gulliver's Travels, 2, 3, 81
Symons, Julian, 85, 86, 87, 88, 89, 90, 92

Thackeray, William, 6
Tolstoy, Leo, 15, 82
Tribune, 66, 67, 72
Twain, Mark, 15, 26, 31, 67

Warburg, Fredric, 43, 70, 74, 80, 83, 85, 88, 89, 92, 93
Waugh, Evelyn, 87, 89, 90, 91
Wells, H.G., xvi, 6, 55, 58, 59, 60, 66, 69, 76, 93
Westrope, Frank, 48, 49
Wilde, Oscar, 11, 67, 83, 86
Wilkes, Mrs Vaughan, 2
Wodehouse, P.G., 6, 74
Woodcock, George, 64, 81, 86
Zamyatin, E.I., 68, 78, 90

3. Places

Barnhill, see Jura
Barnsley, 37
Bramley, 19, 23
Burma, 12, 13, 14, 15, 16

Cranham Sanatorium, 89

Eastbourne, see St. Cyprians
Eton College, 5, 6, 7, 8, 10, 11, 97, 101, 106

Frays College, Uxbridge, 29, 30

Greenwich, 51, 52, 53

Hairmyres Hospital, 85
Hawthorns School, Hayes, 23, 24, 26, 27, 29
Headingley, 37
Henley on Thames, 1, 2, 5, 9, 97

Jura, 75, 79, 80, 81, 82, 83, 84, 87, 89, 95, 96, 98

Liverpool, 36
London
 Canonbury Square, 71, 84, 107
 Chagford Street, 54
 Cheyne Walk, 105

London (*cont.*)
  George Street, 70, 100
  Hampstead, 21, 98
  Langford Court, 58
  Lawford Road, 34, 35
  Mortimer Crescent, 62, 70, 100
  Parliament Hill, 33
  Portobello Road, 15, 104
  University College Hospital, 93
  Warwick Mansions, 32
  Westminster Bridge Road, 23
  Windsor Street, 22

Manchester, 36
Marrakesh, 48, 49, 50

Paris, 16, 17, 18, 72, 73, 102

Polperro, 3, 9, 15
Preston Hall Sanatorium, 46, 48

St Cyprian's School, 2, 3, 4, 6, 108
Shiplake, 3, 4, 7, 8, 9, 97
Southwold, 11, 12, 15, 19, 26, 29, 30, 32, 51, 100, 106
Spain, 40, 41, 42, 43, 50, 101, 102
Sutton Courtenay, 94, 95

Ticklerton, 7, 10, 15

Walberswick, 21
Wallington, 38, 43, 47, 51, 52, 53, 56, 58, 74, 80, 84, 103
Wellington College, 5, 6
Wigan, 36